THE NEIGHBOR'S HORSE

PRINCIPLES FOR REINING IN LIFE'S DIFFICULT SITUATIONS

CHARLIE KESINGER

The Neighbors Horse (Principles for Reining in Life's Difficult Situations)
By Charlie Kesinger

Copyright © 2018 by Charlie Kesinger, The Kesinger Group LLC

All characters and events in this book, other than those clearly in the public domain, are fictitious and any resemblance to real persons, living or dead, is purely coincidental.

All rights reserved. No part of this publication may be reproduced, distributed, or transmitted in any form or by any means, including photocopying, recording, or other electronic or mechanical methods, without the prior written permission of the publisher, except in the case of brief quotations embodied in critical reviews and certain other noncommercial uses permitted by copyright law. [For permission requests, write to [the publisher, addressed "Attention: Permissions Coordinator," at the address below.]

www.thekesingergroup.com

Ordering Information: Quantity sales. [Special discounts are available on quantity purchases by corporations, associations, and others. Orders by U.S. trade bookstores and wholesalers. For details, contact the publisher at the address above.]

Editing by The Pro Book Editor
Design by IAPS.rocks
Interior art by Studio RTP

ISBN: 978-1-7329473-0-6

1. Main category—Business & Economics/Management
2. Other category—Self-Management/Stress Management

First Edition

TABLE OF CONTENTS

CHAPTER 1: *It's a New Day* 9
CHAPTER 2: *Staff Exposure* 13
CHAPTER 3: *Oil and Vinegar* 17
CHAPTER 4: *Wake-Up Call* 21
CHAPTER 5: *Don't Miss the Bus* 25
CHAPTER 6: *The Gift Horse* 29
CHAPTER 7: *Winds of Change* 35
CHAPTER 8: *A Mother's Wisdom* 47
CHAPTER 9: *The List* 53
CHAPTER 10: *The Tides of Frustration* 59
CHAPTER 11: *When "IT" Hits the Fan* 75
CHAPTER 12: *The Human Touch* 81
CHAPTER 13: *Lead, Follow, or There's the Door* 91
CHAPTER 14: *The Taste of Humble Pie* 99
CHAPTER 15: *Delivery* 105
CHAPTER 16: *State Your Intentions* 109
ACKNOWLEDGEMENTS: 113
ABOUT THE AUTHOR: 115

DEDICATION

I would like to dedicate this book to the three constants in my life. First and foremost is to my crazy mom. Without her in my life, I might have turned out normal and missed out on a lot of adventure. Most of all, she has always supported me in my many ups and downs. Second, this is for my two brothers from other mothers. Tommy and Bryan. Their friendship and support never waned even when I was… well, a pain in the butt.

HAVE YOU EVER FELT YOU WERE ON THE RIGHT TRACK ONLY TO HAVE YOUR WORLD UPENDED?

This book is about overcoming struggles and finding answers in unlikely places. This fable demonstrates a series of basic principles that will help provide clarity and lay the groundwork to finding a solution to some of life's difficult situations.

CHAPTER 1
IT'S A NEW DAY

Tommy began his day like most others, enjoying breakfast with his son Bryan and then driving him down to the bus stop. They filled the time they spent waiting for the bus with jokes and banter about their upcoming day, as had been their routine since moving out to the countryside a few years earlier.

Tommy enjoyed his thirty-minute commute through the countryside in the mornings. The fragrant blend of fresh cut hay, steaming coffee, and the occasional cattle drive worked as a special aromatherapy to kick-start his day. The drive to Sanitas Est, where he worked as the vice president of Delivery, always seemed to fill him with the enthusiasm of a child going to play at the park with friends on a sunny summer day. Today was no different as his mind wandered over all that had been happening at work.

The last few years at Sanitas Est had been filled with many accomplishments for both Tommy and his colleagues. They had become a second family for many of the employees, including senior management, who saw their CEO as an older uncle or father figure.

A relatively new player in the software industry, Sanitas Est released a new health registration portal, "SE Dashboard," that had been very successful. The dashboard allowed medical professionals and their patients to gain quick access to insurance pre-authorizations for medical procedures. Medical professionals and patients could log in to the portal to provide the needed information or call into the call center and an agent would fill out the authorization form for them. The new high-speed process to gain payment approval from insurance companies was a huge success, which enabled the organization to offer numerous new perks at the office and extend many of those perks to remote team members as well. The feeling at Sanitas Est was that it was more than a start-up—it was like a multigenerational family business.

A few weeks had passed since most of the leadership had attended an executive retreat with CEO Bart Collins and a team-building group. Retreats were always fun, and this one had been focused on taking the organization to the next level. The current leadership was strong and successful, but it was time for some stretch goals, and most of the company's division leaders were excited to have new performance challenges. A few options were placed up for discussion, and the group decided to bring in a corporate consultant to review their progress and opportunities for improvement and then have the consultant lead them through the proposed changes.

In the weeks after the retreat, Bart took the attendees out for weekly dinners. He enjoyed spending that time with his leadership team and saw it as an opportunity to learn how they were performing. During the workday, they all faced hectic schedules that limited their availability to meet as a group, but the dinners provided a relaxed environment so they could open up without worrying about the time. Last Friday, he'd even offered them all access to the corporate box to enjoy a local baseball game with their families. It was his way of giving back to their loved ones too for their longer work hours over the past few weeks.

All of this was on Tommy's mind as he continued his drive into work. Tommy felt he was in a good place personally and professionally. He was busy, but he paced it well with a clear division between the office and time on the farm with his boy. Their morning routine was something that had just fallen into place when they'd moved into the new house after leaving the city. Bryan loved having room to play and discovering new ways to somehow demolish clothes and keep the dogs covered in either mud or grass. Even at his country oasis, though, Tommy was tethered to the heartbeat of Sanitas Est. As the vice president of Delivery, Tommy managed a global team, so his inbox was under attack all hours of the day and night. He was always in awe at the e-mail mountain that could stack up between when he left his home and when he arrived at his desk.

Today was the day the new consultant was to start, and Tommy was looking forward to the experience. Their ability to review, recommend, and deliver on organizational activities and business goals was critical to pushing the business to the next level. He and his teams had received many awards and accolades for their performance over the past few years, so he assumed the consultant's work would be more of a management exercise to tune performance rather than an organizational shift.

The senior management team had already begun filling seats around the table for the initial meeting with the new consultant when Tommy entered the executive conference room. He filled his coffee cup and settled in with the lighthearted group. After everyone had arrived, the vice president of HR, Alexa Watson, introduced Mr. Mavee.

Mr. Mavee thanked the group and went directly into what appeared to be a canned introductory presentation. It started as do most overzealous infomercials, and a few in the room offered playful jokes in response. Most meetings had always been open to comments and banter as an acceptable way to keep tensions low and camaraderie high. Mr. Mavee, however, was direct and to the point. He was not impressed or even receptive to the management team's history of excellence or their upbeat rapport. In Mr. Mavee's opinion, he was hired to take the company to the next level of performance, and he was determined to be successful. Mr. Mavee drove his presentation straight through the occasional questions from the group, only slowing to repeat how successful he was in his job. The presentation shared little information about how the groups were going to improve or defining expectations other than it was going to happen.

Tommy felt the atmosphere shift right away, soon realizing along with everyone else that this was no simple pitch. It was the makings of something big and very different. And for better or worse, they had all voted for it. The once joyful group looked like someone had just stolen all their holiday gifts as they exchanged nervous glances and took notes.

Many directives were discussed, but very few details emerged as to how they were going to arrive at the grand new results touted by Mr. Mavee. And Mr. Mavee's approach, being so much less friendly and colder than they were accustomed to, had crushed all sense that open discussion and questions were welcome, leaving everyone feeling shell-shocked. The meeting left Tommy confused and concerned, like he'd been dropped into a maze just as the starting gun fired. He couldn't fathom which way to start running.

CHAPTER 2
STAFF EXPOSURE

During his career at Sanitas Est, Tommy had relied on agendas with short, to-the-point action items for Monday meetings and then encouraged his direct reports to manage the expected deliverables. This style of leadership enabled senior staff members to focus on helping their supervisors in a kind of "pay it forward" approach within their teams. Bart had always been a fan of executive leaders grooming their direct reports to elevate their positions, so had encouraged his senior leadership team to work this way since the beginning. He believed this method cultivated strong leaders, offered security in cases of employee transitions, and strengthened the company's overall leadership ability.

Tommy's departments were also well organized with department policies, standard operating procedures (SOP), and flowcharts to provide guidance to team members and those who needed to know how information should flow in and out of his departments. He'd made sure his departments' policies and processes were designed to allow the staff freedom in accomplishing tasks while defining how they received information and passed it on. Mr. Mavee began by implementing changes to personnel meeting agendas and goals and making several recommendations to Tommy about how he should manage his staff, but then quickly transitioned to directing them himself. The changes Mr. Mavee imposed did not follow the methods the delivery teams were accustomed to and had been implemented rather abruptly, with no information to guide a smooth transition.

It did not take long for interdepartmental skirmishes to develop about who was responsible for accepting what tasks and when to pass them to other departments. A steady stream of e-mails with a higher level of urgency than normal began flowing into Tommy's inbox almost immediately, asking for directions or pointing out concerns. Teams that had once relied on structured roles, responsibilities, and proven skillsets now found new gray lines of responsibility that required them to work deep into uncharted areas of their skills and desires. Quickly, the new plan was proving to be more of a melee than a planned action.

At the second weekly meeting following the new delivery mandate, Tommy was trying to get through the agenda when Denise, a longtime member of the team, spoke up. She asked why they were rushing to go over so much information in one meeting and expressed how she and the others had liked the daily stand-ups where they could openly discuss items. Michael, another longtime member of the team and good friend to both Tommy and Denise, was no stranger to telling it like he saw it. He quipped that Denise's concern had more to do with her interest in the free bagels and donuts, which awarded him a menacing but smiling snarl from Denise. Tommy loved the relationship he had with these two. He knew they would always set him straight, and for that, he allowed a little extra leeway to encourage Michael's special talent of delivering his messages.

Tommy had to explain that his approach was all part of a new plan, and the company's new policies included less time in meetings for junior staff, so they would have more time to be productive. The normally energetic group that often laughed and enjoyed friendly banter began to show concern for the abrupt change in operating procedures. Tommy assured them they would work any kinks out quickly, and soon the meeting began to take on the air of friendship and open communication once again.

During the meeting, members of the team exchanged worried

and disappointed glances. Concerns were discussed about how Mr. Mavee chastised members of the staff even when they were following operating procedures. Dean, one of Tommy's top directors, declared that he was not happy with the new employment methodologies and wondered if Bart was aware of the way this new arrival treated his staff.

Tommy felt the emotions building in the room. He knew it was time for a little pressure relief, so he called on Michael to provide one of his famous and often inappropriate jokes to bring the meeting to a close. As if it were preplanned, Michael broke into a joke that poked fun at his dear friend Denise, and the whole group laughed.

It did not take long for Tommy to notice that his once helpful directors were helping less and less with the downstream noise. When he discussed this with them, they expressed their frustration. They were doing all they could to stay afloat, they said, given that Mr. Mavee had instructed them to not work on leadership activities as much and instead work on departmental tasks. The departmental tasks were becoming more than the department leads could keep up with because of the complaining bubbling up from staff about the lack of organizational direction for new procedures.

After about a month, Tommy's growing concern that he and his department were coming apart reached the point where he felt compelled to ask for advice. He didn't feel he could ask Bart, since he'd initiated the changes and might think Tommy was resisting them rather than trying to find his way through. Instead, he asked Karen, a longtime friend and colleague, to lunch. He learned she was having similar issues with her departments and had in fact gotten into a shouting match with Mr. Mavee earlier in the day. She shared that she no longer felt like she knew what was expected from her in the new era. Together, they tried to recall the leadership retreat and why they had all believed there was a need to go in a new direction to begin with.

Karen recalled the great story Bart delivered at the retreat about his personal trainer, Jacky. He'd always thought he was doing what he needed to at the gym, but once he began working with Jacky, he was miserable for the first few weeks and wanted to get rid of her. She made him do things he did not like and pushed him into a better diet. A year and a half later, he felt better than ever. He'd lost weight, was able to stop most of his blood pressure medications, and was about to run his first half-marathon. Maybe Mr. Mavee was just like Jacky. How could we not all want a Jacky in our business life?

Deflated, Karen admitted she was becoming more and more fearful of losing her tenure at Sanitas Est. Tommy consoled her, realizing the same uneasiness had been creeping into the courtyards of his own thoughts.

CHAPTER 3
OIL AND VINEGAR

Back at the office, Tommy finalized the agenda he was preparing for an afternoon meeting with Mr. Mavee. He took a few minutes to enjoy his coffee and notice the many trinkets scattered around his office. At times he could lose himself in all the good memories each little toy or keepsake provided. It was not uncommon for his team or his son to add to his growing collection of miniature trucks, motorcycles, and other fun items. Most recently, a team member had found a toy Harley-Davidson made from little bolts while in India. His attention shifted back to the present as he realized it was almost time for his scheduled meeting with Mr. Mavee.

As the meeting started, Tommy started to outline the information to be discussed.

"We don't have time to cover all this," Mr. Mavee interrupted. "Here is what's going to happen. You are going to get your team in shape, or we are going to start replacing people."

Tommy was shocked. His blood pressure and emotions erupted. "Excuse me! This meeting is scheduled for an hour and a half, and there are concerns we need to discuss."

"Like what?" Mr. Mavee asked.

"Well, for starters, I would like you to take a softer approach when dealing with my staff."

A volley of fire came immediately from all directions, and Tommy, regaining his composure, tried to back Mr. Mavee off the ledge of attack. Mr. Mavee blasted Tommy's team for being weak and incapable of delivering a quality product. He was met by a restrained Tommy as he again tried to regain control of the meeting by prodding Mr. Mavee into explaining his statement that the delivery team was not meeting its goals.

Mr. Mavee again elevated his voice, and this time he slammed papers on his desk and paced erratically around the room. He shouted, "You see, you don't even know what you should be delivering. No wonder you and your team are so worthless!"

Tommy began to feel like a punching bag being pounded by a professional boxer. He began breathing heavily and his hands began to sweat. This type of assault had never been allowed at Sanitas Est before. With a voice of resistance, he asked, "Do you even know what the delivery team does?"

Mr. Mavee was in a rage, acting as if at any second, he would literally hit Tommy. The air in the conference room was beginning to boil from all the body heat pouring into the closed space. Mr. Mavee stared at Tommy like a cougar about to pounce as he addressed the question. "Yes, I know what you do—it's in your title, is it not? You are to deliver products on time. That's why you're the delivery team that does not seem to be able to deliver."

Feverishly, Tommy replied, "Not even close. Seriously, you do not know what my departments do, and you're basing your assumption on my title. We compile or assemble work from other departments into a final product. We don't create code. We make sure its correct to the specification required. If the developers deliver bad code, we send it back so there are no bugs. We are not able to deliver if we do not have the product to deliver. Maybe you should get to know the company better before you become the czar."

Mr. Mavee stared at his prey and slowly sat down, glaring into Tommy's eyes. "I'll clear your team out from under you and replace them with consultants who understand the value of delivering a product."

Tommy asked what the reason was for replacing people. He quickly followed up with information about how his team had been giving one hundred percent, including working fifty to sixty hours a week lately, to try and keep up with the changes and demands that were being created by the lack of process.

Mr. Mavee bellowed, "It's not the amount of time! It's about the amount of *progress*."

At this, Tommy lost his temper. The meeting had lost all focus and deteriorated into a personal assault on his leadership abilities.

"You and your team just do not seem to understand that my plan is going to work," Mr. Mavee explained. "Or that if it does not, there will be personnel put in place that can make it work."

"What is it you need from us that you're not getting?" Tommy asked.

"I really don't know what else to tell you." Mr. Mavee hoisted out from behind his seat and stood over Tommy, looking down at him as he pointed a stern finger. "We are like oil and vinegar, and I don't believe we are going to mix well. If you can't be where I need you, then your people will only be lost following you."

CHAPTER 4
WAKE-UP CALL

With his entire department struggling since Mr. Mavee had taken the reins, Tommy had been spending an increasing amount of time being involved in lower-level details. After working with one of his offshore delivery groups until almost 1:30 in the morning, Tommy realized he still needed to review Bryan's homework. His review done, he lumbered toward the bedroom for what would only be about three hours of sleep.

The next morning, Tommy drove Bryan to the bus stop but asked him to wait for the bus by himself so he could return home and log in to the company network. Bryan was disappointed but knew it must be important by the tone in his dad's voice.

Tommy raced up the gravel driveway to begin preparing with the offshore and US-based teams for the skirmish brewing back at the office. Apparently, two different directors from other areas of the company had demanded that their projects be worked on by Tommy's delivery group per the authority of Mr. Mavee. This break in a longstanding company process caused scheduled deadlines to be missed, and the new work could not be completed owing to a lack of information and resources.

Shortly after 9 a.m., Tommy arrived at his desk to discover a yellow sticky note on his monitor summoning him to Mr. Mavee's office "immediately." As luck would have it, he was also expected in the delivery team's weekly meeting only a few minutes later. Tommy grabbed his laptop and scurried down to Mr. Mavee's office.

Tommy walked in on an already raging storm. Several department directors were venting to Mr. Mavee about missed deliveries while impatiently awaiting Tommy's arrival. Mr. Mavee turned his attention to berating Tommy for being late. Tommy took a deep breath and tried to weather the attack by explaining that he had been working from home to deal with the offshore team's chaos. The more he tried to explain the issues, however, the more tempers in the room swelled. Mr. Mavee raised his voice to a steady roar and demanded that Tommy be in the office for the 7 a.m. calls going forward.

Tommy tried to explain that management was not normally present for this call and that he had logged in to monitor and mentor his junior staff, so in actuality he had been doing more than was previously expected and not been late. He was already in the office about ten hours a day, not counting the meetings and calls he took before he got to the office and after he arrived back home.

Mr. Mavee told Tommy in no uncertain terms that if he was not at his desk before the morning call, he would no longer have to worry about his son waiting for the bus alone. He could be at home with him every day because he would no longer be employed.

Tommy meandered for the door, then looked back and said, "You don't have the authority."

Mr. Mavee quickly rebutted, "You sure about that?"

Having been verbally beaten into silence, Tommy arrived late to the delivery team meeting. The fact that several heated discussions were going on simultaneously made it clear that the meeting would have to be rescheduled once he had time to douse the flames. He tried to call some order to the group, but tempers roared.

For the first time, he raised his voice at the group—his group. "Stop! Stop all of it right now!"

The room went silent.

Methodically, he called on senior members and key personnel to provide updates on issues and concerns. When Michael finished his report, he stood up and sauntered out of the room. No one had much else to say after that. The meeting wound down as Tommy tried to play "company man" and support the new policies and desires of Mr. Mavee even though he felt like he was betraying his own standards.

Tommy had always felt like a part of the team. For the first time, he felt like an outsider.

CHAPTER 5
DON'T MISS THE BUS

The next few days were difficult for Bryan because Tommy had to drop him off early. On the third day, Tommy looked in his rearview mirror as he drove away and saw that Bryan was crying where he'd left him at the end of the pasture. He turned back and climbed out of his truck.

Putting his arm around the boy, Tommy said, "Come on, buddy. You're old enough to be here for a few extra minutes. Besides, it's nice out here in the country."

Teary-eyed, Bryan sniffled and said, "I miss having you here in the mornings, and I get scared." He tried to hold back his tears as he hoped his dad would give in and wait with him.

"Come on, buddy. You are old enough and brave enough to be here for a short time. I trust you, and you know I would stay if I could, but I really need to head into the office. Do it for me and find something to do for the few minutes you have to wait. Try counting the neighbor's cows or goats."

A few moments later he could only watch while his little man teared up as the truck pulled onto the main road and headed for Sanitas Est.

About the time Tommy pulled into the office parking lot, his phone rang. His neighbor's number showed on his caller ID. He answered nervously, expecting to hear that the dogs had gotten out and were playing with the neighbor's goats.

"Hello, Ms. Vanesa. How are you this morning?" he asked, putting on his best happy to-hear-from-you voice.

"Well, that depends on if your little one is supposed to be in school today."

"Sure, he is. It's Friday, right?" Tommy replied. For a moment he'd lost what day it was.

"Yes, yes. It's Friday," she assured him.

"I left him at the front of the property waiting on the bus. Is everything okay?" he responded, reaching for the door.

"He's fine physically, but he had some real concerns about waiting for the bus this morning. He came over and asked if he could help me in the garden. I asked about school, and he said he missed the bus, so he was taking a day off."

Tommy went from worried to troubled and had to hold back from showing his emotions. He thanked Vanesa for calling and said he would be right home to get Bryan.

"There is no need to rush home. I'm good at handling bus-skippers. I can take him up to school, but do you mind if I offer another suggestion?"

"Sure." He felt his blood pressure slowly coming to a simmer.

"If you wouldn't mind, I would love to keep Bryan home today and let him spend some time helping me with the garden. I know it's just you and him, and sometimes it's good for little ones to have someone to stay home and play sick with. And it's Friday. He won't be missing very much today. I'll keep him busy till you get home for work. In fact, why don't you plan on coming over for dinner tonight with Don and me?"

Tommy tried to back out, but Vanesa was not having it. She told him she would see him for dinner, and he thanked her and assured her he would be there by 6 p.m.

Tommy knew she was right. Vanesa and Don Levi were good neighbors with two children. Their son was a little older than him and their daughter was just a bit younger.

After a difficult day of work, Tommy started over to the bakery to pick up some dessert to follow dinner. As he headed over to his neighbors, who were good country folk, he realized the dangers of showing up with a store-bought pie, and after some consideration, he redirected his efforts to selecting flowers instead.

As soon as he turned off the main road, he saw Bryan riding on an old green tractor with Don Levi and glowing with happiness. As Tommy got out of the truck, Bryan bounced up to him exclaiming, "Guess what, guess what?"

"Let me guess, you skipped school today?"

With that, Bryan's energy level fell like a stone, and his eyes began to water.

Tommy scolded him for missing the bus and skipping school.

Don strolled up and came to the rescue of the little rule-bender. He thanked Bryan for all his hard work and asked if he'd told his dad what all the excitement was about.

Bryan looked up at his dad with a flicker of light still burning in his eyes.

Suddenly Tommy realized his son was so excited about telling him some exciting news, and he was ruining some big surprise with his scolding. He felt his belly begin to harden.

"Hey, little buddy, let's put the school stuff behind us, and you tell me about the surprise."

Then, like a blooming flower, Bryan smiled and said, "We're getting a horse!"

"What?" Tommy's face was creased with confusion as he turned to Don.

Bryan continued, "Well, what I mean is that Mr. Levi is getting one, and I helped him get ready for it today. We stacked hay, filled the water tanks, and even made sure there was no sharp stuff around the barn. I also found a turtle that I named Dixie, and we turned her loose in Ms. Vanesa's corn patch."

"Dare I ask how you know it was a her?" Tommy interrupted.

"She peed on me when I picked her up like Nana's dog does," Bryan answered confidently.

They all laughed and headed into the house.

Over dinner, the topic of the horse came up many times. Don explained it was his daughter's doing, and she would be bringing it by tomorrow. She had rescued the animal from an abandoned farm and her place was too small. Don went on to express how his daughter, Mazi, had been dragging animals home all her life. Now, years later, she was a veterinarian and still using their home as the Ark.

As dinner came to a close, Vanesa appeared from nowhere with a hot homemade cobbler. A beaming Bryan explained that he had helped make it, and Vanesa assured him he was a big help and then asked if he remembered what they'd agreed upon earlier.

"Yep, and I won't tell," he said with a sneaky grin.

As they walked to the truck, Vanesa told Tommy he should come by tomorrow and visit with Mazi. She was going to be around all weekend to keep an eye on the new horse. Plus, she got bored after about the first night of just having her old parents around.

Don piped in from the background, "Quit trying to marry off our daughter."

Tommy smiled and said, "It's fine, but I have a lot of work to get to, so I better get going."

Bryan quickly added he would be over tomorrow and make sure his old man came too, then he smiled and ran for the truck.

CHAPTER 6
THE GIFT HORSE

Once they got home, Bryan asked Tommy, "Why don't you get a girlfriend like Ms. Vanesa? She's fun and cooks better than us."

They laughed, and the week's drama slipped away as they fed the dogs and prepared for bed.

The morning was abuzz with "is it here yet, is it here yet" from Bryan. Finally, as Tommy had a lot of work to focus on, he scooted Bryan and the dogs out the door to go find some mischief to get into. As he checked on Bryan a short time later, he could see a serious game of chase was in full swing with the frenzied group circling the barn.

Just before lunchtime, Bryan burst into the house shouting, "It's here! The horse is here! I see the trailer. I'm headed over!"

"Wait," said Tommy. "We'll go over later. I have work to do and you have some makeup homework that's going to get finished before we do anything else. The sooner we're both finished with our work, the sooner we go play. Okay?"

With no debate, a stampede of boy and dogs headed up the stairs. The dogs did not know why they were running, only that when there was running through the house, there was normally excitement to follow.

After eating lunch, Tommy and Bryan wandered over to the Levis' property and strolled around to the front of the house. Bryan pointed out all the places where he and Don had mended the fence and even where they had seen a snake, but they were not to tell Ms. Vanesa about that because "she does not care for snakes," he explained. As they reached the front gate, they could see the horse grazing in the distance, near the main house.

"Come on, Dad, there it is! Come on, come on!" Bryan ran toward where the horse was grazing.

The horse became spooked and retreated into the pasture.

Bryan started to follow when all of a sudden, a commanding call from the house said, "Freeze!"

Bryan froze in his tracks, partially from the command and partially because of the strange voice he had never heard before. As still as a photograph, he stood on one leg with the other halfway through the fence.

After a few seconds, Tommy told Bryan he could move.

Bryan said, "Nooo way. Not until she says it's okay."

They both watched as a lady came out of the house and approached. Tommy quickly introduced himself and his statue-like son.

"I'm Mazi Levi." She shook Tommy's hand, then turned to Bryan. "Are you stuck?"

Tommy said, "Uh, since you froze him, you must unfreeze him."

With a smile, Mazi said "unfreeze" in her commanding voice.

Bryan relaxed.

Mazi knelt down at eye level with Bryan and explained that the horse was scared so they needed to let him adjust. She said they could come back later and try to feed him some carrots.

"Why did it run away? We just wanted to pet it and feed it treats," Bryan said.

Mazi explained, "*It* is a he. And *he* needs a name. He was not very well taken care of and is confused now. So, we have to be careful when we are around him until he understands we are not going to hurt him and we want to be his friends."

With a deflated "okay," Bryan darted toward the house, then stopped and turned back to Mazi. "Can his name be Moose?"

"Moose," Mazi stated. "Why Moose?"

"Because he's so big," Bryan answered.

"Let's wait and see what he likes," she replied with a smile.

Back at his own house, Tommy began slogging through the incoming e-mails and mounting tensions with communications between the US teams and groups in other countries. Throughout the next few hours, Bryan was abuzz with comments about having a new horse next door. Tommy pondered how having a horse nearby could generate that much energy. He smiled as he contemplated how this turn of events could possibly be used to his advantage, like by getting Bryan to mow the yard for the next year. Tommy could not help but laugh to himself.

After many interruptions from Bryan begging to go to the market to get carrots and ice cream for the horse, Tommy surrendered, but he had to ask about the ice cream. Bryan was quick to point out that if Moose did not want the ice cream, he'd make sure it didn't go to waste.

Though they returned to the Levis' farm twice bearing carrots, nothing they did or said would get the horse to come up to them. Mazi explained it could take a little while. Tommy told Bryan it had been a long day and was almost bedtime, so they had to get going anyway. Mazi assured Bryan they would feed him tomorrow. With her assurance, Bryan seemed to settle and agree to head home. He wanted to get to bed so tomorrow would start sooner.

Sunday morning, Bryan was off and ready to see the horse as quickly as his feet hit the floor. Tommy had to corral the little escape artist to make him do his chores and eat breakfast. When they arrived at the Levis, Mazi already had Moose tied up at the barn just down from the main house. Vanesa was on the back porch enjoying coffee, and Don appeared to be tinkering with his old green tractor. Tommy and Bryan went up to the house and knocked at the door.

Mazi answered, inviting them in and asking if they had breakfast.

Bryan quickly replied, "Yep, and Dad burned stuff again, so he had to clean the pans."

Mazi turned to Tommy. "Would you like some coffee that is *not* burned?"

"Please and thank you," Tommy replied.

Bryan moaned, "Aww, man, now I have to wait even longer."

They followed Mazi to the kitchen. The coffee was good, unlike the bargain roast Tommy usually made at home. He could smell hints of nuts and sweetness. He also noticed Mazi was very comfortable in the kitchen and house, definitely a student of Vanesa's. Tommy asked about the coffee and was shocked at the volume of information that could be used to describe a single cup of coffee. He made a personal note to never make coffee for any of the Levis.

After enjoying a wonderful coffee and watching Bryan almost explode from waiting, they went outside and calmly approached the horse. They closer they got, the more skittish the horse became; he was clearly not happy about being tied up to a post. Bryan was becoming afraid to pet the towering horse because up close, it was so much bigger and scarier than he'd imagined. He had been around many domestic animals like dogs and cats and even small farm animals like goats and chickens, but never a horse. After some coaxing from Mazi, he finally fed the giant a carrot. Then he proclaimed he'd had enough visiting with the horse and it was time to let him loose. Mazi did as the boy wished, and the horse ran like bees were chasing him, darting in several directions before settling down on the other side of the pasture.

"Maybe we should call him Wildfire?" Bryan asked.

"He sure seems like his tail is on fire right now, but let's give it some time," Mazi responded.

On the walk back to the house, Mazi expressed concern that her parents were going out of their way to let her keep the horse at their house, but she didn't want to burden them with the responsibilities while she was away at her home and work. She inquired if Tommy knew anyone who would be willing to look after him for the next few weeks until she could find him a home. Bryan immediately raised his hand, volunteering himself and his dad while pulling on Tommy's arm.

"It will cost you another cup of not-burned coffee," Tommy said, shrugging.

Mazi agreed and then led the new horsekeepers around the barn, educating them on the basics of caring for their new friend, which amounted to much more than putting out a bowl of food each night and saying "good boy" when he came running to the dinner bell.

Tommy was a little unsure as to how he was going to pull this off but agreed as if it were no big request.

Tommy and Bryan made their way home and a short time later saw Mazi pulling from the Levi's home, headed down the tree-lined road.

Later that night, Tommy spent several hours trying to corral the horse with no name, although he had given him a few new names in his mind.

CHAPTER 7
WINDS OF CHANGE

It was a bit of a chore getting out of bed Monday morning. Tommy was sore from dancing with the horse and all the extra walking back and forth to the Levis' farm over the weekend. He woke extra early to go feed the horse and let him out to pasture. Even Bryan didn't seem to mind getting up earlier than usual as they went to let loose the horse with no name.

Bryan had brought carrots to give the horse, but when they got there, he wouldn't venture toward him. Tommy put a rope on the gentle giant and led him over to the gate so Bryan could feed him a few carrots, and then they let him loose in the field. After hurrying back to make breakfast, Tommy reviewed his schedule for the workday while Bryan got ready to leave for school.

"Do you have anything else to say about missing the bus and school?" Tommy asked as they rode to the bus stop.

"I'm sorry," Bryan offered. "I won't do that again, but I hate being there alone, waiting for the bus."

"Next time try talking to the horse while you wait," Tommy reasoned.

"I'll try."

All the niceness of the weekend faded as soon as Tommy walked into the office and found one of those little yellow sticky notes on his screen again. He could feel the walls closing in, and his blood began to thicken. He sat down and read the note. It was from Michael, asking to have lunch "off the record" and "off the radar." The "off the radar" part threw him, so he texted Michael and asked, "So, by off the radar, you're wanting to meet me in private?"

Michael shot back, "Yep, and let's keep it between us."

Tommy muddled through the day, dredging through complaint after complaint from different departments and his staff, who were fed up with other departments. After putting out one fire after another, he made his way over to Michael's area and asked him what was up.

Michael said they would talk about it at lunch and asked if he would meet him at Taco Sam's at 1 p.m. In hushed tones, he asked Tommy to not let anyone know they were meeting.

Tommy agreed, a heavy stone beginning to form in his chest. Now he had the added worry of what was about to happen at lunch. Had his longtime friend switched sides and agreed to lure him away from the office so Mr. Mavee could have his office cleaned out while having him fired in a public place? He'd never had these thoughts before. How had it gotten so bad so fast? They had all been so happy just a few weeks earlier. Now he didn't know which day was going to be his last at Sanitas Est.

Time seemed to slow as Tommy waited for lunch. Finally, he headed to Taco Sam's, where he was surprised to see both Michael and Denise waiting in the parking lot. *Sheesh, this is not going to be a good lunch*, he thought. Before he got out of the truck, he felt the stone in his chest form into a boulder. The walk to meet his once-smiling and once-friendly staff, whom he'd always thought of more as friends than employees, now seemed like a walk of shame to the firing squad. After a cordial greeting, they entered the restaurant and asked to be seated outside, away from everyone.

Michael, who was not known for being short on words, went right into what he called the "elephant in the room." "Tommy, we love you, and we have been with you for a long time, but we are at our breaking point. You have always had our backs, even when we were well in the wrong. You have always found a way to pull us together and make us a family. The other day, you turned your back on us and joined the other side."

Tommy started to give his reasons, but Denise raised her voice and took on an ominous tone. "You're about to see the country in me if you don't sit there and listen to what we are saying."

Tommy sighed, then sat back to listen.

Denise said, "You need to write this down, so we brought you some paper. You need to answer some things for us, or we are not going to make it through this. Not just the local team, but offshore is falling apart as well. Most of us have been with you long enough to go through your bootcamps of reading books, playing games, relentless team-building exercises, and driving us to be more than just an employee. You were always reminding us to come into work with positive attitudes, work as a team, and care for each other. We memorized and embodied the mission and vision for you. Now, we hardly see you, and when we do, you're late for meetings. That would have never been acceptable to you before. When did we fall so far down the rung that you don't follow what you teach?"

Tommy sat in silence, letting Denise's accusations hang in the air.

"Let me ask you a question. Do you believe that you and the other senior leaders around here are upholding our values and mission?" Denise paused for a moment to let her question sink in, but continued before Tommy could comment.

"We want to know why we should stay here. What are you going to do to make things better? We are not reading any more books, and we're damn sure not going to do any more team building until we see it, feel it, and live it. And, Buster, you need to come up with what 'IT' is, and I would do it quickly if I were you," she growled.

"Denise!" Michael exclaimed.

"I'm sorry," she replied, "but I have been here many years, and I have never seen it this bad. I can't take much more of it."

"Sorry," Michael said to Tommy in his mocking Southern drawl. "Tommy, we didn't mean for this to come out so bluntly, but I guess the country in Ms. Denise isn't refined just yet." Michael ended his apology with a smile as Denise slapped him on the arm.

Tommy took in the verbal cannonballs and tried to pull a bit more information out from the two about how other members of the team were being affected based on the watercooler gossip. He assured them he was working on ways to formalize the new transition plans as well as find a way to get everyone's work-life balance back to manageable levels. As lunch came to a close, Tommy thanked them for their honesty and reassured them he was working hard to resolve the many issues.

On his way home from work later that day, Tommy wondered what to do about the horse. He was tired, and after a difficult day he wanted to finish up and try and get to bed, ultimately deciding to leave the horse out all night. After dinner, he received a video call from the office to assist on an issue that had passed offshore through other channels but was now beset with problems. The evening time flew by with an avalanche of complaint e-mails flooding Tommy's inbox. With the superpowers only a small child has about asking why and when, Bryan dropped horse questions all evening. Tommy was exhausted and frustrated, and the last thing he wanted was Bryan pressing him about putting the horse in the barn. The final straw broke the barrier of frustration in Tommy when Bryan brought the horse up again instead of heading off to bed as instructed and he boomed, "The horse will be *fine* for the night! Now go to bed!"

"Mazi said he needed to be put up *every* night."

"Not tonight he doesn't." Tommy glared as he muted the video call.

"Yes, sir, but Mazi said—"

"Well, Mazi is not your dad, and *I* say it's bedtime."

"B-but it's not time."

"Now!"

Bryan crept off to bed, head down.

Tommy felt that boulder becoming a mountain.

After about an hour, he told the team he had to go and would be available first thing in the morning to help if needed. When he went to tuck Bryan in, he was hit by little whimpers coming from his room.

"Hey, bud, what are the tears for?" Tommy inquired.

Bryan just looked up and said, "You never used to yell at me. And you always say do the right thing."

"I'm sorry about raising my voice."

"Yelling, you mean," Bryan said.

"Easy now, and get to bed."

"What about the horse?" Bryan persisted.

"What about him?"

"You told Mazi you would make sure he was in every night," Bryan explained. "I'm not trying to make you mad, but the right thing would be to make sure he's home before we go to bed."

"Okay, buddy, you're right, and I need to do the right thing," Tommy said. "I'll make sure he is in before I go to bed. Okay?"

"Sweet. I'm going to feed him with you in the morning," Bryan chirped.

That night, the horse of a few new names was even more determined than usual not to go in the barn. During his tribulations, Tommy learned not to wear his good work shoes in the pasture.

The work week churned on toward Thursday with more of the same long hours and frustration brewing just under the surface for Tommy. As he went to feed the horse with Bryan after dinner Thursday evening, his curiosity about what would happen with the horse grew. He was glad Bryan liked feeding him in the mornings and helping corral him in at night, but all of the chores left little time for much else.

At dinner, Bryan nervously said, "I have a note for you."

"Really? From whom?" Tommy said.

Bryan sat looking down at his dinner plate for a moment before answering. "Well, it's from my teacher, and I don't think you are going to be happy, so I'm going to finish dinner before I give it to you."

"Why do you need to finish dinner before I read it?"

Bryan glanced up. "That way I get *to my dessert before I might have to go to my room.*"

"Bryan, give me the note," Tommy insisted.

"Umm…now?"

"Yes, now."

Bryan pulled a crumpled paper from his pocket and sullenly slid it across the table to Tommy.

The note read:

Dear Mr. Divers,

I want to bring a few things to your attention. For the last few weeks, Bryan's work has been falling well below his normal average. His behavior has also been slipping, as he has become increasingly argumentative with the student aides. This week has been the worst. For three nights in a row, he did not complete his homework and turn it in the next day. I know you are very involved in his schoolwork and are making sure everything is okay. Please have Bryan discuss with you the plan we made for him to turn in his missing work by Monday. Thank you for your continued support.

Ms. C. Reese

As Tommy looked over the top of the note, he noticed Bryan was well into his bowl of his favorite ice cream. With his sheepish demeanor, he looked like a puppy that had just been caught sitting on the family couch. Tommy recalled when he himself had been in this type of predicament at this same age. Bryan sat waiting to hear his fate. After a few minutes, which seemed like eternity to Bryan, Tommy asked probing questions about Bryan's time at school and if he liked his teachers and classmates, as well as discussing homework time. They spent the rest of the night discussing why there had been a slippage, and Bryan agreed to be more focused on work and school.

That night Tommy sat up working, thinking about all that had changed. Life had been so good a few months ago, but since Sanitas Est started its evolution, everything had taken a downward spiral.

The next day was another blur of what was becoming the norm with most of his time spent fighting fires. When he departed the office on Friday, Tommy felt a world of relief that the weekend was here. Even though he would be working from home almost all weekend, at least it would be away from the cubical forest. Stopping off for groceries, he wondered if Mazi was going to be around this weekend and whether maybe he should pick up a few extra items. He got his answer as he pulled into the driveway and noticed Bryan over at the Levis' house, walking with Mazi toward the hay barn. The sight made Tommy tired. He knew he still had dinner to cook and the dance of getting the horse back into the barn for the night.

After putting the groceries away, he headed over to claim his wandering boy. When he arrived at the Levis' doorstep, Vanesa opened the door and announced, "Just in time for dinner."

"No, I couldn't. Thanks for offering, though," Tommy said.

"What do you mean, 'You couldn't'? Get in here. Bryan already started you a plate, and Mazi only agreed to come in tonight if I cooked her favorite meal, so too late for shouldn't and couldn't," Vanesa snapped.

Tommy made his way to the kitchen table.

Don laughed. "You'll learn just to say okay, thank you, and yes, ma'am, with these girls."

After a pleasant dinner, Tommy followed Mazi and Bryan outside to put the horse in the barn. With Vanesa and Don looking on from the porch, the team went to work two-stepping with the horse. They would get two steps forward, then lose a step. Finally, with Bryan laughing, Tommy pulled the horse toward the barn like he had done on many nights, only this time the horse provided Tommy a surprise by stretching out his neck and applying his well-developed chompers to Tommy's shoulder.

"Ouch!" Tommy yelped. "He bit me." That was it! Tommy

dropped the rope, stared at the horse, which seemed to smile back at him, and told Mazi, "It might be good for Mr. No Name to camp out under the stars."

Bryan suggested another new name for the horse. "Can we call him Dracula? Ha-ha-ha!" He ran back to the porch.

Mazi asked Tommy if he and the horse did this every night.

"Only on the good nights," Tommy replied, smiling.

She suggested a break to allow them both to settle down. When they got back to the porch, Vanesa had supplied everyone with some of her refreshing sweet tea.

"You know, I used to chase a girl who treated me like that," Don mentioned.

"Did she bite you?" Bryan asked with a smile.

"Well, she kicked me a time or two."

"What happened?" Tommy asked.

"Well, you can ask her," Don replied as he nodded towards Vanesa and smiled.

"I did bite him, for the record," Vanesa said, causing Bryan to laugh.

"Well," she started, "he was good at chasing me, and I enjoyed the games he would play, but it was not till he made his intentions known and stopped chasing me that I began to follow him like a lost puppy."

"So, what's the secret, Don?" Tommy smiled as he asked.

"I can't tell you. You'll have to discover it on your own and make it yours. Honestly, I believe I just got lucky."

Vanesa smiled with an almost twinkle in her eye and asked, "How is the shoulder doing after becoming part of the food chain?"

Tommy joked and said he thought he would survive, but the shoulder was going to be sore for days. He could also feel the pull of mounting work waiting for him back home.

"It's time for bed, Bryan," Tommy said.

"Aww, man! I wanted to see you chase the horse some more."

"Well, you can watch tomorrow. Come on." Tommy turned to

the Levis and said, "I'll be back in a bit to reclaim my skin from my friend."

With a inquisitive expression on his face, Bryan said to Mazi, "Will you tuck me in?"

An odd sense of quiet fell over the group. Bryan was openly comfortable around other adults and children, but he had never asked to be tucked in by someone other than Dad.

"That's not necessary," Tommy said, feeling a little caught off guard and embarrassed.

"No, please take her. Don and I will put away the raging pony," Vanesa responded. "I don't want to risk any more injuries to the neighborhood."

The group laughed again as they said good night.

Tommy led the way down the meandering dirt trail between their properties, enjoying the familiar aroma of cut grass and fresh flowers as Bryan bounced Tigger-like and tugged Mazi along.

After Bryan was all tucked in, the adults retired to the porch. They noticed the horse was in the corral already and joked that even the horse didn't argue with Vanesa.

Mazi asked Tommy, "What exactly do you do for Sanitas Est? I know it's IT or something, but I'm not sure."

"I manage the delivery side of a software group. I have nine departments that work together to compile other departments' code into a usable single product. We take code from developers all over the organization and test it for security holes, bugs, and usability. If any of it is bad, we return it and help them understand what is below par or broken. It's kinda like a newspaper or magazine. There are many different people writing different sections, and my departments pull it together, proof it, and get it to the reader, or user. "

"It takes nine different departments to make all that happen?" Mazi questioned.

"Yep, and we have groups around the world, so we can pass the work on to keep it moving forward 24/7. A group may be made up of different departments, but they work as a cohesive team. For example, group A will pass work to group B when group A goes home. Then group B will similarly pass the work to Group C when it is the end of group B's shift. Group C will do their part and finally pass it back to the group here in the USA. Group A and C meet at seven in the morning each day. This allows us to get about three days' work completed per twenty-four-hour cycle."

Mazi said, "That's a lot of touch points per day."

"You're telling me. It's like a global game of hot potato." Tommy shook his head and sighed, looking off into the distance for a moment. Turning to Mazi, he said, "Would you like a glass of wine, or a beer, or…?"

Mazi glanced at her watch. "I need to get back to visit with Mom a bit, or she will have a reason to have me up with the morning sun Thank you for helping out. I know you have a lot going on, and this is not your normal kind of stuff. I really do appreciate it." Mazi stood and headed for the stairs off the porch.

Tommy watched as she made her way down the trail, following the driveway into the little darkness between the two properties. A short time later there was a flicker of the Levis' porch light, signaling her safe arrival.

Saturday was a mental train wreck for Tommy. Work invaded almost every thought. The offshore groups were imploding because the new workflow channels were demanding high priority on non-prioritized work. The local teams' time was being swallowed up by meetings trying to determine why so much code was failing and being sent back to have bugs removed or resolved. There was also the matter of Bryan and his homework to contend with before Monday.

While on a walk down to get the mail, Tommy spotted Mazi in the pasture. He grabbed the mail and then walked over to the fence and invited her to come experience some bachelor-style home cooking later. She offered to come over about three in the afternoon to visit and help out around the kitchen, but Tommy pushed for five-thirty, so he could help Bryan with his homework, including learning a song for an upcoming play, in which Bryan would be singing with his classmates. She inquired if she could come over around four to see what homework was like for little people these days. Tommy's head was reeling from thoughts of the impending work disaster, burning out of control and waiting for him back at the house, so he smiled and acknowledged 4 p.m. would be fine.

Bryan got his homework finished in record time and magically put up no fuss when Mazi reviewed it with him before dinner. Mazi watched in wonderment as Tommy did not burn down the kitchen while preparing dinner. Bryan, always quick on his feet, was able to get in a few shots about burnt eggs before running for cover and being summoned to set the table.

CHAPTER 8
A MOTHER'S WISDOM

Monday night after dinner, Tommy and Bryan went to put the horse with no name away for the night. As they were finishing up, Vanesa came outside and asked, "Would you guys like some dessert after all your hard work?"

Bryan didn't need to be asked twice, so they delayed the trip home to enjoy some treats with Don on the porch.

After cookies, Vanesa asked, "Tommy, could you come by tomorrow about the same time and bring your truck?"

Don spoke up. "Don't worry about it, guys. I will move whatever she needs moved." Then, turning to his wife, he asked, "What is it that you're moving?"

"This doesn't concern you, fella," Vanesa replied.

Tommy grinned and said, "Don, this might be one of those 'okay' times."

Don chuckled and nodded his head, returning to his attention to the plate of cookies.

The next day, Tommy and Bryan showed up after dinner in the truck. Bryan was singing along with "A Country Boy Can Survive" by Hank Williams Jr. on the radio, which he would be singing in the play with his classmates in a few days. Mazi had helped him select it, steering him away from "Life Is a Highway" by Rascal Flatts and "Party in the USA" by Miley Cyrus.

Vanesa climbed in next to Bryan and asked if they could drive to the barn. On the way, Tommy told her about how Mazi had helped Bryan select his song. Vanesa shared that Mazi had loved to listen to Hank Sr. when she was growing up, particularly his song about a wooden Indian who loses his love, and she would play it over and over. "She used to act it out in our living room," she chuckled. "I don't know the other two, but if there is a Hank song in the mix, it will always win, even if it is from Junior."

When they arrived, Tommy grabbed a handful of hay.

"Why do you take hay out to the horse?" she asked.

Bryan explained that they fed him to get him to come to the barn.

"Does it work?" she asked.

"Sort of," Bryan blurted out. "He comes to eat the hay, then we have to get a rope on him, and Dad can pull him to where we want him."

"Hmm. Can we try something different tonight?" Vanesa said.

"I'll try anything," Tommy said.

"Well, let's put the hay in the feeder, sit out here and call the horse, and offer a few carrots."

"You're joking," said Tommy.

"Nope," said Vanesa. "Let's sit on the tailgate and listen to Bryan sing his song."

"Well, okay," Tommy said.

Tommy restarted the song and turned up the music a little, then joined Vanesa and Bryan on the tailgate. In between Bryan's bouts of singing, they called the horse by clicking and offering up the sweets. After about the same amount of time it would take for them to chase the horse around the field and get him to the barn, he came up to get the carrots. Vanesa walked him gently to the hay waiting for him in his stall. They all returned to the house, and Vanesa asked if she could listen to Bryan practice his singing again tomorrow night at the same time.

"You bet," Bryan answered.

Tommy just smiled.

By the end of the day Tuesday, work had become almost physically unbearable. Most of the meetings consisted of team members yelling at each other. Yelling was becoming the norm between departments as well. Tommy was trying to lead both his onshore departments and his offshore groups with common goals and policies, but synergy was becoming impossible to achieve as demands were hitting the groups from all angles and becoming unmanageable. Tommy felt the pressure was starting to affect his health. He was always sweaty at work, and his chest and head felt as though they were being squeezed in a vise throughout most days.

Tommy's normal beating from Mr. Mavee graduated to a full lashing as a company project was now officially off track. All fingers were pointing at different areas, but the common theme was that the delivery team was responsible for deliveries. Tommy tried in vain to explain that the delivery team relied on other teams for their ability to schedule and deliver products.

"No, no, no! It is your responsibility to get this done. Is delivery not in your department's title?" Mr. Mavee questioned.

"That's not fair!" Tommy exploded, feeling he was being blamed for the fault of other people and for failing to foresee the difficulties other departments were having.

"If you want fair, go to a schoolyard. Now get out of my office and get this fixed!" Mr. Mavee shot back, a glistening of sweat starting to show on his forehead.

Tommy left for the day and visited his doctor to address his mounting chest pressure and headaches. The doctor asked more questions than normal, then gave Tommy some serious news: He had developed high blood pressure and was going to need to start medication right away, or he was sure to have a stroke or heart attack. He had also started to put on weight.

Tommy was beaten and couldn't take much more. As he made his way to his truck, he thought that when it rains it pours. He paused in his reflecting and grinned as he mentally changed the word "pours" to "becomes a hurricane." He left the medical center for home with a new bag of pills in tow.

That night, Tommy and Bryan picked up Vanesa; Tommy drove his new horse-wrangling team to the barn once more. Along the way, they enjoyed Bryan singing "A Country Boy Can Survive" over and over. Vanesa asked Bryan if he thought he would reach his goal of learning the song before having to sing it at the school show on Friday. Bryan proudly answered, "Sure I am," and asked if she would attend the event. Before she could reply, the horse materialized like a ghost seemingly out of thin air next to the truck, and Vanesa asked Bryan if he could help with feeding and clearing old hay. Tommy watched as Bryan fed the horse carrots and walked the meandering giant into his stall for his dinner. The horse was beginning to show up on his own, and Bryan was easily being led to do more work.

Tommy had a moment of clarity and a tingling feeling that something was at play, but he could not detect just what it was as he took in a little more detail about what was transpiring around him.

On the way back to the house, Vanesa encouraged Bryan to practice every night, then said, "I would love to listen to your progress every night before feeding the horse, if that would be okay." After a short moment, she smiled and offered, "Let's make our own little goal and make it our intention to beat it. I'll come on Friday and bring a date or two if you can sing the song to me by Thursday night with just the music."

"Deal!" Bryan chirped.

Tommy felt like there was something larger at play than Vanesa was letting on, but he agreed to be there tomorrow with Bryan at the same time.

The week progressed with Bryan's singing improving and the horse arriving a little earlier each day. On Wednesday, Vanesa told Bryan that she'd better inform Don they had plans for this Friday. Bryan beamed with pride and confidence.

On Friday, Vanesa kept her word and brought Don and Mazi with her to Bryan's performance. Tommy took a seat close to the Levis and waited for the big moment. Bryan took the stage and sang like a champ! He knew every part of his song and smiled from ear to ear.

After the show, they all went to dinner at Bryan's favorite restaurant. Tommy offered to put the horse away even though Mazi was available to do it. After dinner, the group headed to the Levis. Vanesa asked if they would mind driving to the pasture, so she could tag along for an encore of Bryan's singing. When they arrived at the barn, the horse was already making his way under the shelter.

Mazi was shocked. Bryan had become used to the horse showing up on time, so he just broke right into his song as Tommy put the horse in the stall with fresh hay. On the ride back to the house, Mazi asked what had happened, and Bryan explained that since they started showing up, playing Hank every night, the horse had started coming up on his own.

"Really," she answered back. "Well, maybe he is a fan of Hank Williams."

"That's it! We should call him Hank," Bryan said. "Maybe he likes Hank better than Dracula."

Mazi agreed and asked Tommy and Vanesa what they thought.

"If that's the case, he'd better not bite me any more," Tommy said.

"Hank will be a great name," said Vanesa.

CHAPTER 9
THE LIST

The next morning, Tommy headed over to let Hank out as Bryan finished his homework. He gave Hank a few extra treats for not biting him and to thank his new friend for making Bryan happy. Then a little light started flickering deep in the back of his mind. He headed up to the Levis' house, where Don greeted him at the door and offered a cup of coffee.

"You know, that's just what I need," Tommy said, following Don into the kitchen.

Vanesa looked up from tidying up after breakfast and asked, "Tommy, are you here to see Mazi?"

Tommy responded, "No, I'm here to see you."

"Hey, you trying to steal my girl?" Don joked.

Tommy jested, "Yes, but only for a little bit."

Vanesa gave Tommy a cup of coffee and a pastry and then followed him out to sit on the porch.

After a short silence, Tommy said, "I'm trying to figure out how you did it."

"What?" Vanesa asked.

"How did you get Hank to come to the barn by himself every night? Also, I had been trying to get Bryan to learn his song, and you had him eating from your hand."

"Now, Tommy," she started, "a mom can't give away her secrets to just anyone, you know. You might use them against me." Vanesa gave Tommy a warm grin that lit him up inside.

"I feel you have some insight to what has been going on with Hank and Bryan. It's as if you have things figured out before they happen," Tommy said.

Vanesa watched the deep concentration sweep across his face.

Tommy went on to tell her all about what had been happening at work and how he was struggling to make it work at the office, but somehow knew she could help. The issues were escalating to a point where he just didn't know how to align his teams with the business's new mandates.

Vanesa didn't respond immediately to his question about work. Instead, she asked what he thought they had done so far with the horse and Bryan.

"Well," he replied, "I'm guessing the trick with Bryan was that you led him to where you wanted him to go by allowing him to believe he was getting what he wanted, which was for you to come to the school show. You added a stretch for him to have the lyrics memorized, so he would have to really work on it, but I don't know why since they were going to have the songs and lyrics playing in the background."

"Yes, I upped the ante without him knowing because he was caught up in the moment," Vanesa explained. "He knew he could secure what he wanted and was confident he could do it. It was an easy win for him. I got him to state what he wanted. I reminded him by letting him know I had better make plans to be at the show. And I made sure to show I was involved and invested by coming to feed Hank with you. It was the same for my little ones at that same school."

Tommy paused for a second before responding, "Okay, but what about Hank?"

"Well," she said, "that is a little more complex, but I followed the same steps. Do you know what they are yet?"

Tommy looked perplexed. "Um, well," he fumbled. "No, I don't know."

She said, "Let's walk through it. First, we showed up every night at the same time and in the same place. We rewarded Hank for coming to us by giving him treats. We did not give him treats for just standing there or making us come to him. We needed him to come to the barn. We showed him this is what we needed him to do by rewarding him for his consistency. Before long, he understood our intentions, which was to feed him and secure him for the night. He expected he would receive his treats as a form of rewarding positive behavior. Now we have to keep it up and simply continue the treats while looking for more ways to help Hank understand what we need from him."

Tommy looked a little confused but began to see everything had been part of an orchestrated series of events. "Okay," he said. "So you have a step-by-step cookbook?"

Vanesa smirked as if she were about to get caught for something.

He continued, "I don't believe this is the first time you've led school boys to thinking everything was their idea, all the while you were guiding events to a desired conclusion."

"My mom also taught me a woman never tells," she replied, and they both laughed. "Let's review, and I'll make it simple for you to remember."

"It's important to announce your intentions and inform others of your goals and what your expectations are. Be consistent with your actions, show you are sound in your conviction by demonstrating to others you have a direction, and encourage them to come along. You need to reward positive behavior and let others know you notice their accomplishments and appreciate their efforts. Make sure to reflect on how things went by reviewing what worked and what to improve in the future." Vanesa slowed her speech to make an impact as she stated, "Remember, there is always room for improvement."

Tommy sat taking it all in, then after several moments he said he needed to test her recommendations out to see if they would work universally.

Vanesa suggested they should look for a simple test. "What would be something that would help in the short run?"

Tommy thought of Bryan's sadness over waiting for the bus alone in the mornings. Discussing this with her made it even clearer in his heart that he needed to fix that. He concluded that the answer was in finding a way to not go into work so early, but Vanesa asked if there were other approaches to resolving the issue.

"No," he said. "I just need to put my foot down at work."

They sat there for a moment, watching the trees sway in the comforting breeze.

"What else is there, Tommy?"

He looked as if he were digging deep. His thoughts were still around work, and he began discussing a big project that was going south. Without further prompting, he began to describe all the moving parts at Sanitas Est and how its departments and teams were at complete odds with each other.

Patiently, she listened and then asked, "How's Bryan doing in school and settling into living in the country?"

"The poor boy's loving the outdoors, but we are struggling with chores, schoolwork, and playtime for him and me both. Our lease is coming up for renewal, and we can't decide where to live."

"Well, if I can make a suggestion: have you ever heard the saying 'happy wife, happy life'?"

"Sure, but as you know, there's no Mrs. Divers."

"True," she said, "but that also can mean 'happy home, happy life.' Is your home happy right now?"

"It's not all bad. We're just a little stirred up at the moment."

"Well, Tommy, I would focus on something where you can monitor your behavior first. Once you're comfortable with the steps, let's broaden the experiment. If we were going to work on something that would make your home better, what could it be?"

"Winning the lottery," he said with a smile. "Seriously, I believe if I can get Bryan and me on the same page every day and keep a few things from falling behind, it would really help."

"Okay. Now, what is your intention? Let's think of it as a purpose or mission."

"I like the lottery idea better."

"Come on, now, give me your intention."

"Okay, my intention is to provide a better way for Bryan and me to keep our lives in step and for me to be able to focus on tasks at hand."

"There you go. Now remember what we discussed and make it happen. Here's a recap of the things we went over:

- **Announce your intentions** – Let others know your goals and what you expect.

- **Be consistent with your actions** – Show you are sound in your conviction by demonstrating to others you have a direction and encourage them to come along.

- **Reward positive behavior** – Acknowledge and reward when you see positive behavior.

- **Reflection** – Review what worked and what to improve in the future.

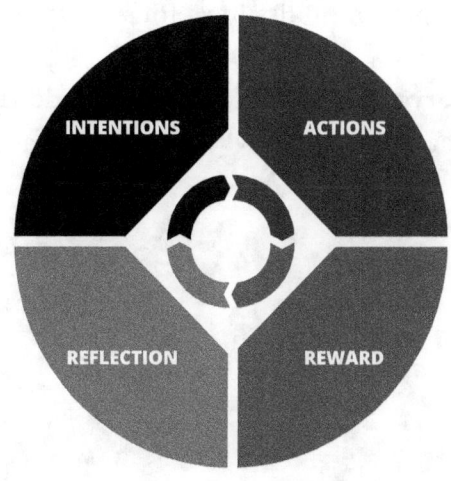

"Once you get through this with improving your daily routines, let's look at a problem that's a little bit larger, okay?"

"Sure," he said with a crooked smile, wondering if he had just gotten himself into more than he was ready for with his already overflowing plate.

That night, Tommy asked Bryan if he wanted to start earning some allowance. Allowance had been a long-time wish of Bryan's, but Tommy had always said he was too young. Bryan was all too eager and expressed his willingness to take on a thousand chores. Tommy said they would start slow and build from there to be sure Bryan learned how to balance both his homework and chores. He laid out two tasks for school, two for home, and two bonus tasks.

The first school task was to make sure all homework made it home and got completed daily. The second was to get the homework back to school and turned in on time. The two tasks for home were to take out the trash on trash days and feed and water the dogs daily. The two bonus tasks were to let Hank out every morning and put him away on Tuesdays and Thursdays.

"No problem," Bryan said. "When do we talk about the pay part?"

"Well, you think about it and tell me what you think is fair. Do it for a few days, okay?"

"Sure, but what are you going to do?"

"I'm going to pay the bills, look for a new house, and do my chores."

"Is that all?" Bryan asked. "It looks like I'm doing more."

"Well, little man, let's see how this works out and maybe we will trade."

CHAPTER 10
THE TIDES OF FRUSTRATION

Monday morning, Tommy reminded Bryan of his tasks over breakfast, and in Bryan's usual, 'I got this' manner, he said, "No problem."

The morning moved along smoothly, allowing them to leave for the bus stop early enough so Tommy could get to work before his 7 a.m. call. Still, despite the promising start, Tommy's workday did not begin well. The morning call was a mess. There was leadership from other areas of the company unloading their frustrations on Tommy's offshore team. The offshore team was doing their best to explain the process that must happen before new code is published and tested, but the new wild, wild west way of dumping untested code on the offshore team was clogging the system. Several times, Tommy tried to step in and explain that new projects needed to come through the pipeline and not just jump to the front of the line. Each time Tommy would start, someone would announce "by the authority of Mr. Mavee." Then it became a contest as to who could speak over each other among department heads. Luckily, time ran out and the call ended.

At his second meeting of the morning, he found himself facing the firing squad during the weekly team meeting that had fully transitioned from a focused gathering into a complaint session. The number of complaints about other departments set a new all-time high, and their issues were complicating the delivery of an upcoming yearly release project. Tommy tried to maintain a calm demeanor and lay the groundwork for a compromise, but the room only spun further out of control, with people interrupting and talking over one another.

Some in the group were very vocal about their feelings on the changes in both their working environment and operating procedures. There were also silent glares that either burned right through Tommy or gazed off into the distance. Many team members looked like frightened rabbits just waiting for the cage to open so they could dash to the forest and hide from an impending thunderstorm.

After the meeting, Michael and Denise visited Tommy's office to express concern about the upcoming yearly release project. There were mounting issues with the project, including bugs in the code that needed to be fixed. The overall quality of the work being delivered to the team was very poor. They were very far behind in receiving essential deliveries and didn't see a way to make up the time while allowing their departments to properly test the deliveries, return bad code to the developers, and retest until it was correct. Michael desperately wanted someone to let the business stakeholders, including senior management and the departments expecting the software, know the projected dates were in trouble if they wanted a quality product. Denise raised a concern that if the project did not get the proper testing, the delivery team would be on the hook for any issues clients found in production.

Tommy offered a genuine expression of gratitude after they had finished, thanking them for taking the time to come to his office and share their concerns. In his normal manner of "don't just bring complaints, also bring solutions," he asked if they had any suggestions to help solve these concerns.

"Sure, just tell them it will be a different delivery date or they are going to get a crap product," Michael replied. "Remember, good sir, like the picture behind your desk says: High Quality – Quickly – Low Cost; you are the one who says you can only pick two of three ways to deliver a product. Ask them which two they would like." He flashed a halfhearted smile as he left the room.

Tommy sat there looking at the picture Michael referenced and all his office memorabilia from past corporate events, fun times he'd had with his team, and keepsakes that people had given him when they returned from vacations or adventures. The veins in his neck and jaw tightened, feeling as if they were passing molasses. It was time for his blood pressure to begin its daily climb.

Later that day in Mr. Mavee's office, Tommy tried to carefully discuss his team's concerns about the delivery dates and the quality of the work going into the release.

Mr. Mavee lashed out at Tommy, telling him he was easily one of the worst leaders he'd had to work with, and it wouldn't be long before he didn't have to worry about Tommy's incompetence anymore.

Tommy, taking it on the chin, responded in a calm manner, "Why is it you seem to dislike me so much and are so adversarial?"

Mr. Mavee got right to the point: "You do not deliver on what I tell you to do."

Tommy's cool demeanor began to unwind as his temper and emotions quickly erupted. "What do you mean I don't do what you tell me to do? I have been picking up the pieces of my departments, and many of the others, since you've been playing boss and destroying years of hard work."

Mr. Mavee proclaimed that he would be taking over next week's meeting with the teams and ordered him out of his office.

Tommy spent the next two days trying to identify the missing parts of the yearly release project. Heading home later than usual, he called Bryan to let him know he would pick up his favorite food as a treat. He pulled into his driveway as the sun was just beginning to set. Hank was still out in the pasture and Bryan was riding his bicycle up and down the driveway as if he were racing a motorcycle.

As Tommy drove closer, Bryan yelled, "I'll race you, Dad!" and off he went up the gravel drive, toward the house.

Tommy revved the engine as if he were about to start a race, but of course, Bryan won. In preparation for dinner, they headed for the kitchen table. Tommy stuck to the house rule that all meals were to be in the kitchen or dining area even on takeout nights. Bryan loved to test this rule by trying to eat on the run or sneak treats into the TV area. There would be no sneaking tonight. They joked at Bryan's stumbling to use chopsticks with his steamed rice and dumplings. Tommy liked seeing him tackle the challenge of using chopsticks. Soon, discussion of homework and chores bubbled up.

Bryan waited until his dad was finished talking, then hung his head. "Well, funny you should ask. I have a note from my math teacher for not turning my work in today."

"What?" Tommy looked directly at Bryan. Calmly but firmly, he said, "I helped you with it last night."

"I know, but I forgot it on my desk in my room."

"Come on, buddy, you have to get it back to school. This is important, and it's one of your tasks."

"I know. I just forgot."

"Did you forget Hank as well?"

"Aww, darn it! I did! Can you do it tonight?"

Tommy slowly shook his head no.

"Man, Dad. It's already dark now…"

"Nope, buddy, these are your chores. I tell you what, I will sit on the porch while you go do it."

"Pleeeeeeeease?" Bryan begged.

"Nope, not going to happen. Come on, let's finish up and check tonight's homework."

A short time later, Tommy sat on the porch reviewing his own To Do list. He realized he had not paid a few bills on time and was going to incur some late fees. *Ouch.* That night, while tucking Bryan in, a discussion came up as to who should receive credit for the horse chore.

"Sadly," Tommy began, "I don't believe you should receive a reward since I had to remind you to do both schoolwork and missed chores."

Pouting, Bryan asked, "Did you do *your* chores?"

"Well, most of them," Tommy replied.

"How do I know you did?"

"You just have to trust me."

"That's not fair."

"Why?"

"Because I always trust you, but you aren't trusting me."

"Yes, I am. You just made a mistake and did not get the chores done. You can do better the rest of the week."

"I still don't think it's fair."

"Well, let's see how the rest of the week goes. Okay?"

Bryan made one of his signature expressions that revealed he was focused on something. "Okay, Dad. Love you."

The next morning was a fresh start with Bryan shooting off to visit with Hank and letting him out of the barn to explore the pasture. Tommy and Bryan finished breakfast, then headed out for the school bus stop and work. Tommy had to maneuver around a few tree limbs that had recently reached the driveway and threatened to scratch up his truck, and he made a mental note to take care of it when he had time. When Tommy got to the office, Bart asked Tommy and Mr. Mavee to visit with him in his office. Tommy dropped his things off at his desk and headed over.

Once the men arrived, Bart expressed his concerns about the yearly release project.

Mr. Mavee assured him that there was no reason to worry. "All of the departments have been completing their work and getting it over to Tommy's delivery group, which has the responsibility of completing this on time," he explained.

"The delivery team doesn't bear the full responsibility of making projected dates, nor the quality of other divisions' work," Tommy interjected.

In response, Mr. Mavee began openly chastising Tommy and his departments. He railed against the "mountain of insubordination" that the delivery group displayed and their perceived lack of quality leadership.

Tommy kept trying to speak but was talked over by Mr. Mavee. His efforts to make sure Bart knew the other departments were delivering bad code that did not work and was clogging up the pipeline, and the delivery team had to continually keep sending it back for patching, seemed futile.

The meeting was not going as Bart had planned but listening to the two go at each other helped him begin to understand some of the rumblings of discontent coming from his lower divisions. After allowing the battle to continue for some time and hoping it would peter out, he intervened. "Tommy, please prepare a presentation on the status of the project. Include the incoming flow of work, expected timetables, and a critical issues list for a stakeholders' meeting. And, guys, please cool the emotions and bickering tones before the meeting and show some unity."

Over the next few days, Tommy focused on how to help the other departments get their information ready for the presentation. With only four weeks to go before the project was scheduled to go live, when the employees and customers would be using the new software, he knew long days and nights would be needed to even remotely be successful in making it past the finish line. Tommy also tried to lower expectations and shorten the number of features to be put in this release. It was his hope that he could convince or prepare others for a limited release that would only have core features and then introduce the additional features at a later date. His campaigning didn't go unnoticed by Mr. Mavee, who was visibly upset that people seemed to be preparing for failure. Tommy tried to explain his reasoning to Mr. Mavee: that he felt they needed business to prepare an emergency plan while understanding ways to turn off the changes that were not critical.

Tommy worked closely with his teams to keep the fires from distracting them and helped with communications between divisions. Both Thursday and Friday were grueling, and his head was constantly under pressure as if it were simply about to pop.

The project manager, Ben, spent many hours developing revisions to timelines, classifying projects as either "work completed" or "work yet to be turned over to the teams for testing." One of the new issues they had never really confronted was the amount of work coming into the Deployment department's work queue. Much of it was simply far below par and had to be sent back to the originating department for reworking. This rerouting meant testing had to start over, and additional testing was needed for coding where it interacted with other functionality. To make matters worse, code testing was a tedious and time-consuming process.

As the weekend approached, there was a feeling that the ship was beginning to move in the right direction. The fear of not getting to the scheduled completion date was on everyone's mind, but the mood was shifting to fight rather than flight. Tommy's team was trying to fight and push toward a common goal. There were those who were at their breaking point, but Tommy's leadership style ensured people who needed him were kept close.

On Saturday, while reviewing Bryan's weekly homework report and chores schedule, Tommy realized that they had both missed the mark about remembering their chores during the week. He offered a trip to get a treat so they could brainstorm about what would help them focus. As they enjoyed their scoops, Bryan mentioned that if things were written down so he could see them every day, it might help.

A few brain freezes later, they visited an office-supply store and picked up a new whiteboard and a pack of twenty colored dry-erase pens. According to Bryan, the four- and ten-packs were for people who had limited imaginations; Tommy didn't want to debate this logic.

At home, Tommy and Bryan worked together to mount the whiteboard in the hall. Recalling what Vanesa had told him, Tommy wrote out her list of instructions but customized for the duties at hand:

- **Announce your intentions**
    - By next weekend, we will both complete our daily tasks.

- **Be consistent with your actions**
    - Every morning we will remind ourselves of what is due daily and/or what's due for the week.
    - Every evening we will check to make sure we completed our tasks.

- **Reward positive behavior**
    - Bryan can stay up 30 minutes later each night his tasks are complete.
    - Tommy gets to kick the soccer ball as hard as he wants down the driveway each night his tasks are complete, and Bryan must fetch it.
    - The midweek reward is dinner out, also known as "Boys' Night."
    - Completion reward: Bryan = $5, Tommy = a trip to get his truck washed.

- **Reflection**
  - Next Sunday, we will reset and adjust goals as needed.

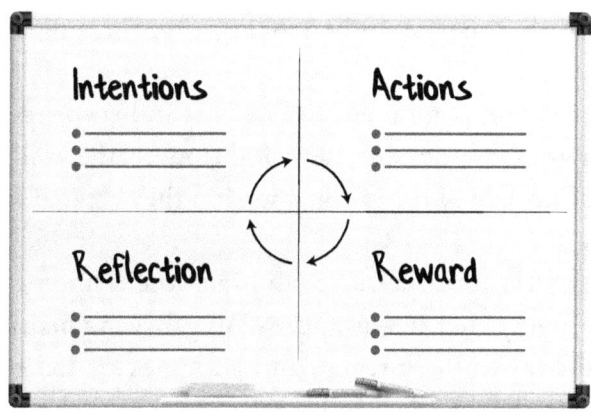

After dinner, Bryan noticed someone walking up the driveway. He and the dogs sprinted out to the wraparound porch to see who the invader could be. Recognizing Mazi, he lit up like lightning had run through his little frame. The dogs lit up in turn from the energy bouncing off Bryan and began to run around as Bryan made his way around the porch to the stairs and down to the lawn.

Mazi high-fived Bryan and followed him as he guided her up to the house. The dogs were still close by because there would surely be more excitement. She greeted Tommy with a smile and a comical "Hi," as Bryan still had her in tow all the way to the main area of the house.

Once anchored on the loveseat, she announced that she had stopped by to see how things were coming with the boys and offer Bryan a treat for taking care of Hank. Then she magically produced some large tickets, explaining the tickets were to attend a traveling country fair that was visiting the area in a few weeks.

"Sweet!" Bryan proclaimed.

Tommy smiled and said, "Is this a ploy to get Bryan to take care of more animals?"

Mazi laughed and said, "Maybe."

Not skipping a beat, Bryan added, "Maybe they will have elephants!"

Mazi assured them there would be no elephants, just farm animals, but that she would enjoy watching Tommy tame an elephant. She also explained that she would be looking after the animals when the fair was in town.

As if there wasn't a moment to lose, Bryan beckoned Mazi down the corridor to show her the new addition to the wall. Mazi and Bryan added the date of the fair in a section they created titled "Don't Forget."

The night critters were beginning their nighttime opera, reminding Tommy that it was approaching Bryan's bedtime. After a bath, several trips to the kitchen, and a long excursion to locate the dogs, Bryan strolled by Mazi and asked, "Are you tucking me in?" He had developed a habit of getting Mazi to tuck him in whenever she was around.

While she was tucking him in, she said softly, "Maybe for next week's reward we can add a behind-the-scenes tour, if you get all of your tasks done."

Bryan sat quietly, and she could see he was very focused. After this pause, he said, "But what about Dad?"

"Well…let's make him clean some horse stalls, if he doesn't complete his tasks."

They both laughed. She dimmed the lights, and they wished each other a good night.

Come Monday, Tommy thought about all of the work he had done over the weekend and how things at home seemed to be getting better. He enjoyed his morning ride through the country to get to the office, but slowly the fog of war began to settle in as he approached the building. After settling into his office, he headed to the department conference room for the morning kickoff. Thankfully, Mr. Mavee never showed as he had threatened, but Ashlie from HR sat in.

The tide of complaining was approaching its normal level until Ben's new charts, graphs, and timelines made it clear to everyone exactly where they were on the project they were discussing, helping to focus their energy on productive discussions. The charts included what the originally projected completion date was, the revised date based on the current pace of work, and how many working hours it would take to finish the testing and certify the product was complete and ready to use. The graphs also outlined the completion rate of the outstanding work, which was coming in at a steady climb of about 45 degrees, meaning it was going to take at least ten more weeks of hard work from the departments outside Tommy's areas.

Ashlie asked why the deployment team wasn't fully responsible for the product's deployment.

Michael, waving his hand in the air like a schoolboy who knows the answer to a question on the big test, explained, "The Deployment group is made up of nine departments who receive the individual contributions from about ten different departments within the organization that are not reporting to Tommy. We assemble the parts and test that they all work together. If any of the individual contributions don't work properly, the deployment teams send it back to the group that provided the code with instructions about what needs to be fixed, then that particular department has to fix the errors and resubmit their work to us, and the whole process has to start over again."

Denise could tell they were losing Ashlie, so she stepped in and said, "Let me put it in English for you since Michael likes to talk too much. Think of a book that has ten chapters and each chapter has a different author. We act like an editor and put the book together, then read it. If a chapter does not fit the story or just isn't good, we give it back to the person who wrote that chapter and ask them to fix it. Then, we have to reread it again to see if it fits into the book properly yet."

Ashlie laughed and said, "Thank you, Denise."

"Oh, you just wait until lunch," Michael said to Denise.

The room laughed for the first time in a long time.

Ben completed his presentation by explaining that to hit the desired target date, the graph would need to be so steep that it would look almost like a vertical line.

Later that day, Tommy presented the information to Bart, Mr. Mavee, Ashlie, a few department heads whose departments would be using the software, and a few concerned board members. With some caution, he advised that they move the date out or reduce the number of deliverables for the yearly release project.

Bart was visibly concerned about the project being so off track. It was not typical for a project to be this far off its scheduled delivery dates or for there to be so much difficulty moving it along. He expressed concern for the end user who might end up with a software package that was below the standards they had all worked so hard to adhere to in the past.

Tommy began to explain. "The changes in the operating procedures and policies are colliding with the major release schedule," he said. "In hindsight, maybe we should have finished the annual release project and taken a step-by-step approach to rolling out organizational changes."

Mr. Mavee abruptly stood up, waved his hands in Tommy's direction, and pointed to the door.

Tommy just stood there looking a bit confused and trying to regulate his emotions. It was unprecedented for anyone presenting in this type of meeting to be so boldly and awkwardly dismissed.

Bart instructed Tommy to stay and for Mr. Mavee to provide his observations and recommendations.

Mr. Mavee continued standing but did not begin to speak until Tommy had taken a seat. He began by tearing the presentation apart and making accusations that called on numerous unsubstantiated facts, focusing on the fact that the delivery group provided the original timelines and arguing that they were now blaming others for their own shortcomings. Again and again he circled back to the phrase "delivery is in their name."

Tommy yet again denied the problems were his team's alone but emphasized they were owing to a range of issues surfacing from across the organization. He said, "A year ago when we started this endeavor, the timelines were based on formulas proven year after year to be correct."

"Why, then, can you not make your deadlines *this* year?" Mr. Mavee asked, his body positioned as if he were delivering a killer blow.

"It's like making good cookies. You follow the recipe," Tommy answered. "When you follow the same recipe and have the same variables, you should get the same results. If you begin to change the variables, you might end up with better cookies or you might ruin the whole batch. What I do know is that it's best to experiment with the recipe in small batches before you enter the year's biggest competition, so your biggest effort is your best. We changed everything about our recipe and variables right before our largest delivery of the year, all at one time, and without really explaining the changes to anyone doing the baking."

The room fell quiet; it was as though the air was being siphoned off.

"Your little story may be a fine excuse for first-year managers, but a senior professional should be able to overcome and deliver what they are told to deliver regardless. You are failing miserably," Mr. Mavee replied, looking confidently at Bart. "This is why you can't grow the company. You have an incompetent management team who are both lethargic and insubordinate."

The officers of the company asked Mr. Mavee what he felt they should do.

Mr. Mavee sprung into action, declaring that the dates for delivery were fixed in stone as far as he was concerned, and Tommy should be released from the organization at once.

Tommy's heart sank, and he began to feel sick to his stomach. Time seemed to slow to a crawl.

Betraying a touch of anger in his voice, Bart declared, "No one is going to be proposing someone's release from the organization today, and this was not the time nor place for such comments. Mr. Mavee, have a seat. We are going to table this group meeting until next week as far as the dates go. I would like Mr. Divers to meet with both HR and our company grievance officer to discuss the information from this meeting and the other meetings happening throughout the day."

As they left the meeting room, Mr. Mavee cheerfully told Tommy, "It won't be long now. You may have Bart covering for you and trying to make me look bad to the rest of the executive team, but even he won't be able to save you."

It took everything Tommy had to not engage with Mr. Mavee at that moment, but he'd worked with Bart for many years and trusted him.

Tommy went to his office and called an emergency meeting with his department leaders to explain what was needed for the rest of the week and ask that they show support for the idea. The plan was not an easy sell, but he explained that it would show what they could do under extreme circumstances. For most of the team, the hours of work were going to increase greatly, the stress was going to become elevated even further, and their communication abilities with other departments outside their areas of influence were going to be strained and tested. It would require around the clock work from each team member and all hands on deck from all the offshore groups as well. Meals and refreshments would be supplied. This all hands on deck emergency push would provide a good baseline to test Ben's assumptions on what was possible to deliver if the group was truly operating at 100 percent capacity. This process was going to be akin to holding the gas pedal on a car to the floor to see just how fast a car can go.

Ben said he was worried that they could do this for a few days, but not for seven-plus weeks.

"I know, but we need a best-case baseline as to where we are now and what's even possible," Tommy replied.

Once there was an agreement on the plan, all the other department directors, leads, and various people involved with the project were called together to explain what needed to happen. A few departments from other areas of the organization definitely did not buy in and were very resistant to do more than what they were already doing. Finally, after some skillful deliberation, negotiation, assurances, and a few big IOUs, those not directly under Tommy's leadership reluctantly agreed to offer *some* support, while all of Tommy's department leaders agreed to show their full support for the next few days. For the rest of that week, including Saturday and Sunday, the teams pushed for 14 to 16 hours a day while the offshore teams were working closer to 17-hour shifts. It was grueling and required a lot of focus. During the weekend, Tommy had food delivered to those that wanted it. He even made personal visits to some of the local team members' homes to thank them, and he brought cards or flowers for their family as an apology for keeping them separated during this time. The weekend was a blur with everything going on at work.

Mazi came over for a bit on Saturday to help Bryan with homework and provide distraction so Tommy could focus on work. She invited Bryan to accompany her to the feed store on Sunday to purchase supplies for Hank. When they returned, they had takeout for Tommy and, based on the ice cream stains on Bryan's shirt, he knew there had been a stop by the sweets shop.

After dinner, Bryan said he wanted to review the board while Mazi was there. They all made their way down the hallway, and Bryan launched into a full explanation that he had check marks by all his tasks and even the bonus ones, but Dad was missing a few. Mazi and Bryan giggled as if they had a secret and Tommy was being left out.

"Okay, what is it? I'll have to add more to mine this coming week."

"Nope," Bryan said slyly. "You get a consequence."

"Oh, really?"

"Yep!"

"What is it?"

"Mazi will tell you after I go to bed!" Giggling, Bryan ran up to his room, calling the dogs.

Tommy and Mazi watched in amazement the amount of energy Bryan could summon before bed and the command he had over his canine companions. After the rustling calmed from the bathroom and the assault on the bed frame was complete, there was a call for Mazi to come up and please tuck him in.

CHAPTER 11
WHEN "IT" HITS THE FAN

On Monday morning, Tommy felt like he was ready for the coming week. His team had worked all weekend to produce the best possible results under the extreme circumstances. He had a great morning with Bryan, and they'd reviewed the new board together before leaving the house, setting off their week with a feeling of being organized.

Bryan had made his own section on the whiteboard for a project he and Mazi had cooked up.

It read:

- **Announce your intentions**
    - To teach Hank to wait at the bus stop with me.
- **Be consistent with your actions**
    - Every morning, give Hank treats for walking down to the bus stop.
- **Reward positive behavior**
    - If Hank is at the bus stop in the afternoon, he gets extra treats and three cubes of the new super treats from the feed store.
- **Reflection**
    - What worked?
    - What did not work?

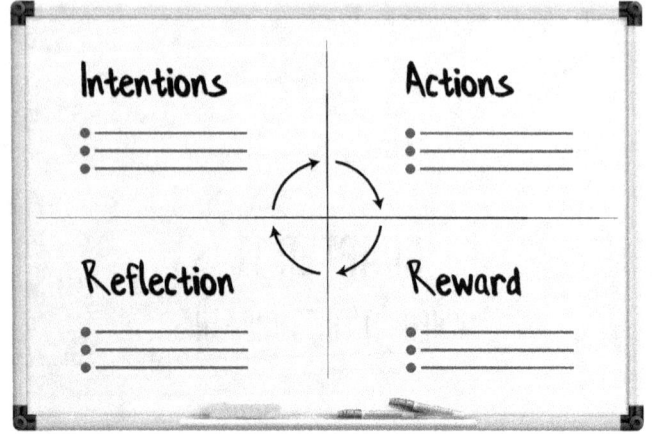

As Tommy started to climb into the driver's seat of his truck, Bryan asked, "Dad, can I walk down to the bus stop alone?"

Tommy asked, "You're not planning another skip day, are you?"

Bryan smirked and said, "Nope, I just need to visit with Hank on the way."

Tommy made a motion like he was going to mess up Bryan's hair and then gave him a big hug instead. After climbing into his truck, he made his way to the main road, avoiding those pesky tree branches he needed to cut back, as they seemed desperate to drag the top of his truck.

For the first time in a while, Tommy felt like things at home were beginning to refocus. They were not out of the woods yet, but the magic Vanesa had helped him understand was beginning to show results. Bryan was doing well in school, and their home life was more than pleasant—it was downright enjoyable.

Arriving at the office, Tommy assembled his team and began by thanking everyone for working wild hours and maintaining a positive and supportive attitude. Ashlie from HR attended, and she also thanked the teams for their effort and dedication.

Next, it was Ben's turn to speak. He discussed the areas where work needed to be completed by other departments. There were a few outlier departments who fell under different vice presidents who had been a bit difficult to network with, so Ben explained that the information would be streamlined and shared with Bart and those who needed to take action within their areas of the company. Overall, the mood was calm, and Tommy's team was working as a unit again.

As the meeting was winding down, Mr. Mavee arrived. His demeanor was stiff and he seemed to be in a big hurry, his hands clinched and fidgety. He started by blaming the team for all the long hours other departments had to work, stating, "The incomplete areas of the project were a direct result of the failing delivery division."

Tommy felt the room return to the over-pressured, explosion-pending state it had been before their department had pulled together as a team over the past week. His heart pounded as he watched the reactions in the room.

Mr. Mavee threatened everyone with their jobs if the coming weeks didn't go flawlessly and everyone did not continue giving the same extended effort and hours until project completion. If anyone had issues with the hours or what was expected, he could have new people sitting in their desks within a few days, he assured everyone. Then, as if a bell had signaled the end of a class, he marched out of the conference room and down the hall, leaving Tommy to take the volley of attacks and glares he'd left in his wake.

Tommy's high hopes for pulling the team together evaporated, and now he just hoped to make it out of the room alive. By lunchtime, he received a message from Bart to attend a mandatory meeting with HR at 5 p.m. Back in his office, Tommy looked again at the many mementos from happier moments in his and his team's lives over the years. As he glanced around the room, he noticed a photo of him and Bart from one of the many company outings. They were standing together and smiling as if they had just won the lottery. Is it possible that his longtime friend and mentor had been swayed by Mr. Mavee to let him go? The thought created a feeling much deeper than sadness in him, something more akin to real dejection. He could feel a little tingling in his belly and a slight wave of nausea threatened. Tommy felt like he was really going to be fired. The astonishment was more than he could bear. Yet again, his veins seemed to be filled with molasses.

A few minutes later, a meandering flow of employees dropped by to deliver their Notices of Separation. Some quit on the spot and others gave notice. This was not unexpected, but Tommy was shell-shocked nonetheless. Never in his career had something like this happened. Tommy and the delivery team were spiraling out of control and falling fast. This meltdown was a new low for Sanitas Est and his professional career. Most importantly, he was failing as a friend to those he had worked with and cared about for years.

Tommy shut his office door and thought of cleaning out his desk. Then he thought of Vanesa's recipe.

- **Announce your intentions** – Let others know your goals and what you expect.
- **Be consistent with your actions** – Show you are sound in your conviction by demonstrating to others you have a direction and encourage them to come along.
- **Reward positive behavior** – Acknowledge and reward when you see positive behavior.
- **Reflection** – Review what worked and what to improve in the future.

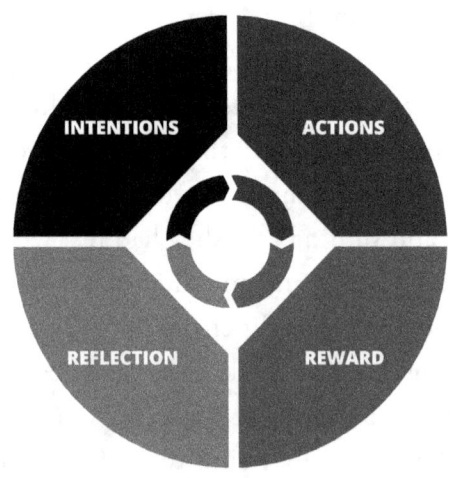

The watercooler talk on the company messaging application was describing an exodus going on after most of the department meetings went horribly amiss throughout the day. Tommy thought back on his morning and could only imagine that same scene playing out over and over throughout Sanitas Est's meeting rooms. He knew the offshore teams better be ready for a tsunami of unpleasantness.

Tommy began by asking himself, "What do my intentions need to be to solve this?" He knew he needed to break it down into bite-sized initiatives and feed them to the group to get momentum going in a single direction and eliminate the noise.

A few minutes before 5 p.m., Tommy went to meet with HR and the grievance officer. He stopped by Bart's office on the way to ask him to dinner. Bart looked as if he'd had a long difficult day as well.

"Hey, old man, you good?" Tommy inquired in a halfhearted poke. "I know it's short notice, but it's a bit of an emergency for the company, I'm afraid."

"Tommy, are you asking me to dinner to quit?" Bart asked gently.

"No. Are you sending me to HR to have me fired?"

"No, I need your help to figure out this mess."

"Then come have dinner at my place tonight, so we can work on a plan," Tommy offered.

"Okay. I'll be there about seven if you make steaks."

"See you tonight."

Tommy left Bart's office relieved that this was not going to be his last walk to *that* side of the building, at least not today. He kept going over Vanesa's four steps and how he might be able to use them. With newfound confidence, he decided to go on the offensive. He would provide direction that people could relate to and believe in.

CHAPTER 12
THE HUMAN TOUCH

Ashlie and her supervisor, the VP of HR, Alexa Watson, invited Tommy to the small conference room in the HR department for their meeting. Ashlie thanked Tommy for coming to visit even though it was a request from Bart, then began telling Tommy that she'd already informed Ms. Watson about what she'd been witnessing lately, including the uncomfortable meeting a few days back with Bart and other senior leaders in which Tommy was sent from the room. Alexa then asked Tommy to explain why *he* felt there had been a flood of resignations in the last few weeks and more on that day than on any day before.

"Alexa," he said, "how long have you known me?"

Unsure of where he was going, she answered, "For a few years."

"Ashlie, how long have you known me?"

"Well, I believe a few years as well."

"Okay. In all that time, have I been requested to visit with either of you because of my performance or for misconduct?"

They both quickly shook their heads no and tried to assure him they were just trying to find a way to resolve the mounting issues at the company. Alexa asked if Tommy would list ten things he believed were important as a leader of the organization.

Tommy used the dry-erase board to make the following list:

- Lead with and foster trust.
- Nurture staff and develop an understanding of the human side of our workforce.
- Hold everyone accountable to the mission and values of the organization.
- Teach and mentor rather than demand.
- Share in success.
- Support individual values and growth.
- Make it safe to explore and fail.
- Support and enforce a code of conduct.
- Build strength through fellowship.
- Remember to play.

Alexa and Ashlie took many notes while Tommy was writing out his information on the board and providing a narrative to each point. Alexia asked him, "Do you feel we as an organization have been meeting your top ten?"

"We used to," Tommy answered.

"Why do you feel we don't anymore?"

Tommy sat there for a few moments and took a drink of water. "I believe it began to change when we decided to retool our processes." He was careful not to get into the blame game—there would be a proper time to identify weak points and disruptive employees.

The group continued discussing the number of people who had left and were looking to leave. Both Alexa and Ashlie wanted to know what Tommy felt could help turn the company around. He informed them he was meeting with Bart for dinner and had a plan, but needed to discuss it with him first.

With a laugh, Alexa said, "Tommy, are you sucking up to Bart for a big promotion?"

He smiled and said, "An hour ago I thought I was on my way out. There's no kissing up here."

They all agreed to meet again in a few days after Tommy had some time with Bart and was able to process more information. After this thoughtful conversation with Ashlie and Alexa, it was time for Tommy to head home and prepare for his dinner meeting with Bart.

The sun provided a picturesque backdrop for the farm as Bart's car pulled up the long driveway. The sedan was not accustomed to being off the smooth city streets, nor was Bart used to driving on dirt and gravel. On more than one occasion, the car spun its tires. Tommy went out to the front porch to greet his guest, as did Bryan and his parade of dogs.

Bart climbed from his car. "Now I see why you drive a monster truck," he said. "I would not be able to get up this driveway in the snow or heavy rain."

Tommy appreciated the attempt at banter, but thought Bart looked tired and beaten. "Yep," he said, "it keeps corporate types at bay. It's my country moat. Come on in. I'm about to throw the good stuff on the grill. Can I get you a glass of tea or water or a beer?"

"Nothing right now, Tommy. You can tell me about your idea while we wait on the steaks, though," said Bart.

Tommy replied, "Why don't we relax a bit, until after dinner, then discuss work?"

Bart replied, "Well, things are pretty serious, so I was hoping to begin working on the issues sooner than later."

"A compromise then. No work talk until we sit down for dinner. The remainder of grilling time was to be work-free, but after that, we talk shop. The down time will do us both some good, Bart. Agreed?"

Bart agreed, and the longtime friends stalked the grill, waiting for their dinner. Tommy made small talk, trying to keep it light as they enjoyed the cool evening and view from the porch. Having waited patiently for the grownups to leave room for him to join the conversation, Bryan asked Bart if he had heard about their horse.

"No, I have not. Did you get a horse?"

"Well, kinda. His name is Hank," Bryan said. "He lives next door, but Dad and I take care of him. Maybe you can come meet him after dinner."

Bart commented on the clean smell of the countryside and the great smell coming off grill.

Bryan chimed in, "Just don't go to the barn. It smells a lot different in there."

By the time they sat at the table with the grilled steaks sitting center stage, work discussion had momentarily slipped Bart's mind. When the meal was nearing completion, Bart asked about Tommy's invitation to talk.

Tommy grinned and asked Bryan if he could put Hank away tonight so he and Bart could "talk about boring grown-up stuff."

"Sure, but it will cost you two scoops tomorrow," Bryan replied.

"Deal!" And as soon as dinner was over, Tommy and Bart headed to the porch while Bryan raided the refrigerator for carrots.

Tommy and his guest meandered out onto the large deck that wrapped around the house. After some further small talk, the discussion began to focus on the issues back at the office. Tommy described what he had observed since Mr. Mavee had been brought on and what he'd discussed with Human Resources. Bart was listening but watching Bryan work with Hank.

Realizing he didn't have Bart's full attention, Tommy asked, "Are you okay?"

"Sure. I'm just amazed Bryan went to feed the horse in the dark, and the horse came to meet him like it did. Has the horse always been so well-trained?"

With that, Tommy laughed out loud till his eyes were tear-filled. "That horse was the bane of my existence. I fought that horse every night for weeks. He has kicked me, stepped on me, and even took a bite out of me. I don't believe he liked me one bit in the early days."

"Really? You must be joking."

"No," Tommy replied. "We even called him Dracula before we named him Hank, since he bit me."

"How did you train him?"

"Well, it's more like how was *I* trained," Tommy replied.

"I don't get it."

"Let me explain…" Tommy recounted the story of how the horse had come into their lives and that while getting to know his neighbor Vanesa better, she'd led him to train the horse without his really knowing it.

Bart watched and listened intently.

Tommy was explaining how he'd put this approach to the test in his own house when Bryan came flying past with the dogs on his heels.

"Bryan, what are you doing, bud?"

"I'm feeding the dogs, but I have to beat them to the barn."

"Why?"

"That's how we do it."

"When you're done, come back to visit, okay?"

"Sure," Bryan replied, and off he went again.

Tommy turned back to Bart and explained the four steps Vanesa had taught him.

- **Announce your intentions** – Let others know your goals and what you expect.
- **Be consistent with your actions** – Show you are sound in your conviction by demonstrating to others you have a direction and encourage them to come along.
- **Reward positive behavior** – Acknowledge and reward when you see positive behavior.
- **Reflection** – Review what worked and what to improve in the future.

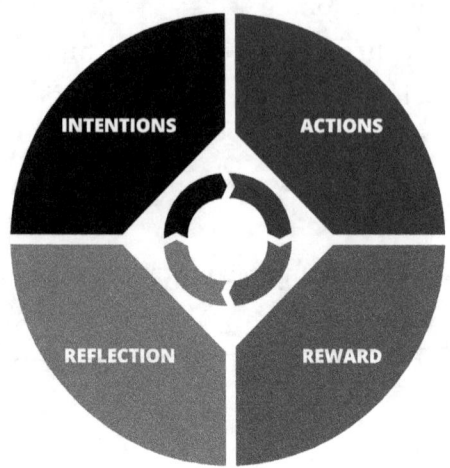

"This sounds like a lot of business philosophies, like Deming, Shewhart, or ITIL," Bart replied.

Tommy nodded his head in agreement. "But there's one main difference."

"What's that?"

At that moment, there was a ruckus happening on the porch and it was headed their way.

"Let's ask Bryan."

With the grace of the scarecrow in *The Wizard of Oz*, the gangly boy bounded on the scene with his pant knees much dirtier than when he'd left.

"Hey, bud, what happened to your pants?"

"Nothing. They're fine."

"What's on the knees?"

"Just dirt."

"Oh," Tommy replied, looking over to see Bart amused, so he left it at that.

"Buddy, can you show Mr. Collins the whiteboard and explain it to him?"

"Sure."

The group followed Bryan inside and down the hall to the other side of the house. Once there, Bart noticed the dry-erase board broken up into sections and with decorative drawings around the edges.

Bryan began explaining what Bart was looking at. "This drawing is of my dogs, and this is Hank, and—"

"Not that part, Bryan. The writing parts," instructed Tommy.

"Oh, okay. We have four steps to our tasks. Step one is what we want to do. Step two is making sure we stay on track. Step three is we get treats for doing good. Step four is we talk about what was good and bad about our tasks. We try and have some of both the good and not so good, so we get better next time," Bryan explained. "This side is mine and Dad's for the week. This area is for Mazi and me. We are trying to teach Hank to meet me at the bus stop."

"Mazi?" said Bart.

"The neighbor," Tommy interjected.

Taking it in, Bart asked, "How is it all working out?"

"Today was the first day teaching Hank, so he came down with me in the morning, but when I got home he wasn't waiting for me," said Bryan. "But he did come and walk up the driveway with me, so he got his super treat for that."

"Well, that was a very good explanation, Bryan. Thank you, and I'll make sure your dad is out early enough tomorrow to get you those two scoops."

"Thanks, Mr. Collins."

Tommy said, "All right, buddy, get ready for bed, and I'll be up later."

Bryan made it all the way upstairs and then yelled out, "Good night, Mr. Collins!"

"Good night, Bryan." Bart turned to Tommy. "Do you remember having that much energy?"

Tommy chuckled, and stood listening to the sounds from upstairs another few moments. After the rumbling upstairs slowed, Tommy and Bart made their way back to the dining room table.

Bart said, "I believe I see where you are going with this. This plan is not about project management; it's about people management."

"Exactly," Tommy agreed.

Over the next few hours, the two worked at the kitchen table discussing how the company and the staff had gotten so off track. They worked the four steps backward and found they had good intentions, but steps two (be consistent with your actions) and three (reward positive behavior) were lacking.

"Can I ask a few questions?" Tommy asked as they worked. "I'm not trying to belittle, but I need to ask."

"Of course. What is it?"

"Can you tell me the company's mission statement and values?"

"Are you serious?" Bart asked.

"Yes, I am."

Bart started reciting, but quickly realized he was getting them wrong. "Man, it has been so long since I reviewed them."

"How about the yearly release project—do you remember what it is? I only ask because it's our largest release and affects every customer we have. I don't expect you to know the code, but do you know what it is and what is going to be affected?" This one really stung, and Tommy saw he'd hit a nerve. "I'm sorry, Bart, but as your friend, I need to ask the tough questions and point out when your zipper's down, like you once said."

"No, I didn't."

"Oh, yes, you did. You told us a friend would giggle if you came into the room and your zipper was down, but a real friend would tell you and then tease you in private."

"Well that sounds like some motivational stuff I would say, so I'll give you a pass."

"Then can I ask another question?" Tommy asked.

"You might have used up your question queue for the day."

"What if your zipper is still down?"

"Man, you're killing me. Let's have it."

"Do you know, at a strategic level, if we have current position descriptions, department charters, and workflow graphs?"

"No, I don't, but to be honest, I don't feel that at my level I need to know all of this," Bart replied.

"I agree, but do you know if they're even in place, so the people who *do* need to know the information have it? I'm not saying you need to know the position description for the developer in the Coding department, but shouldn't you be confident that the right person has that information and the developer is being led in a way that makes sure they're the most successful they can be for both their personal growth and the organization's success? Truly pardon my abruptness and delivery, but how can you lead the ship if you can't tell others why and how you're leading?"

"Ouch. Is my zipper up now?"

"Yep."

"Well, I think I got my junk stuck because that hurt."

"I only tell you because I care," Tommy said.

They were both feeling the effects of a long day, a big dinner, and the late hour.

"It's getting past my bed time, I'm afraid" said Bart. "How about we start back at this in the morning, back at the office?"

Tommy paused, noticing he was definitely feeling the battles of the day. "Tomorrow sounds like a good idea. I know you have a lot on your plate and your time is important, but I believe we are making good progress."

Bart asked, "Do you believe we can fix this and right the ship?"

"I do," Tommy responded. "I really do. We just need to rework our approach, get buy-in, and foster trust."

Bart thanked Tommy for dinner and the late night of productive work and reminded him he had better make time for Bryan's treat.

CHAPTER 13
LEAD, FOLLOW, OR THERE'S THE DOOR

THE NEXT MORNING STARTED EXTRA early. Tommy and Bart each had several meetings to attend and needed to prepare for a mandatory leadership meeting after lunch that they had called. Tommy spent the morning with his team and those directly linked to the yearly release project, while Bart was largely meeting with operations. Tommy felt energized and optimistic about the prospect of getting the organization on track. For the first time in a few weeks, Bart seemed to have some extra pep in his step, supporting the reawakening of his convictions.

As Tommy sat in his office fueling up on coffee and preparing for his presentation, there was a knock on the door. Following Michael's patented tap: *tap, tap, tap—tap—tap, tap,* two visitors stuck their heads in the room.

"Come on in," said Tommy. "Hey, guys! What's up?"

"We need to talk. Can you come to lunch?" Denise asked.

Tommy felt the reoccurring sense of dread building in his chest. "Guys, last time we went to lunch, I thought I was going to get mugged," he tried to joke, but there were no smiles back.

"We're serious. The delivery team is in real trouble. The offshore team is in chaos because no one is following protocol about submitting work to be tested, and the onshore team is getting code releases mixed up as people are just jamming in code to get it off their plate," Michael said.

"I'll tell you what. You put your trust in me until next week. If I disappoint you, I'll buy you dinner and pay for a happy hour."

"Okay, free drinks," Michael said, quick to answer.

"No, Michael," Denise said. "We need to talk to him today."

Tommy stood up, walked over, and hugged Denise, telling her he knew she was looking out for him but asked if they would hang in there just a few more days. Tommy assured them he was getting ahead of the speeding train and would have something to report soon.

The two visitors nodded agreement as they made their way out. Michael said, "Top shelf. Not the cheap stuff."

Tommy smiled, glad he could count on Michael to make him chuckle even in the most difficult times, and got back to work. After lunch, he made his way to the mandatory leadership meeting, tapped into the fresh coffee, and looked over his notes until the rest of the attendees arrived. As they filed in, Bart strolled in behind the main group and made his way to the front of the room.

The meeting was called to order, and Bart addressed the room. "Folks, we are here today to discuss something I learned last night. I do not have all the answers, and I do not know how we are going to do it, but I believe we can make this happen." He made eye contact with each person in the room, seeming calm, confident, and humble.

"I have been with Sanitas Est for a long time. The leadership and staff have supported me through prosperous and lean times. Never have we lost control until now. I say we are in the middle of a raging forest fire. Everyone in this room operates as our lead firefighters in times of crisis like we have now. So, I have a few questions for everyone here. They are going to be tough, and I can guarantee most in the room will feel awkward and maybe even frustrated before we are finished. But please stick with me through this exercise."

Bart took a deep breath and let it out, then continued.

"Now, before we start, I want to tell you what a nine-year-old boy taught me last night." He glanced at Tommy. "Last night I went to dinner at Tommy's, which, by the way, is not easy in a car. After dinner, I watched a little boy in a neighboring pasture *at night* lead a huge horse across that pasture. That horse was hundreds of pounds heavier than him and towered over him, yet that little boy was in full control, and he later explained to me that he was even expanding on his control by teaching the horse to do things even when the boy wasn't there to check on him. So, I asked this little fella how he did it. You know what he said? He said you must let the horse know what you want him to do, trust he will do it, and then reward him for good behavior. Sounds simple, doesn't it? I had to wonder if this little guy knew something about business and what we were missing."

Bart paused for effect and to allow others to visually imagine what he had described. "So, with that, I would like Tommy to come up and go over what he and I discussed and lead us all through this part of the meeting."

Tommy calmly arose from his seat and made his way to the front of the room. On his way up, he handed Ashlie a stack of papers and asked her to distribute them. "I have prepared six questions. Please review them and write your answers on the paper Ashlie is distributing." Trying to lighten the mood, he quipped, "No cheating. These are to be answered by only you, so please don't discuss the answers."

The questions on the paper were:

1. *What is the company's mission statement?*
2. *What are the company values?*
3. *What is the purpose of the Yearly Release Project?*
4. *Do you have current position descriptions for every member of your team?*
5. *Do you have a department charter?*
6. *Do you have current workflow diagrams to illustrate how your branch runs and interacts with the other divisions?*

Once everyone had finished, Tommy said, "Let's see how we did. Can everyone please stand? Come on, I know we just had lunch, but let's get some blood flowing."

"Really? Are we little kids?" Mr. Mavee blurted out.

"No, we are not children," Bart replied. "We are the leaders of this company, and if anyone wants to leave the meeting, please feel free to do so now."

With that, everyone quickly stood up, including Bart.

"Okay, this is how it will work," said Tommy. "If you get the question correct, you can sit down." Then he began. The projector broadcast the mission statement on the screen.

"Feel free to have a seat if you got it right," Tommy instructed.

There was a moment of awkward silence, and Alexa sat down.

"I got it wrong last night as well," Bart said.

Tommy led the group through all six questions and, as he progressed, only one or two would sit down for each question.

After all the questions had been reviewed, Ms. Rays, a vice president of Programming, spoke up and said, "With all the work we have to do, isn't going over this basic HR type of stuff a waste of time?"

Mr. Mavee stood up. "Look at all the wasted salaries in this room. You are all the top earners at Sanitas Est, and you're squandering the morning going over basic management stuff as if this were a college presentation." Mr. Mavee looked at Bart and then to the other attendees.

"Well, Ms. Rays and Mr. Mavee," Bart began, "of the six questions, how many did you get right?"

Ms. Rays proclaimed that she ran a division of more than two hundred people and did not need Tommy questioning her about things like the mission and vision statements.

Mr. Mavee joined in by saying how he got the warm and fuzzy stuff, but reminded Bart that, in his own words, "there was a raging forest fire."

"You are exactly right," Bart added, "and if we are all the lead firefighters, what does it tell you if we can't get the six basic principles of our attack right? Most of us didn't even get the first two answers, which is why we are all here. So you and Ms. Rays want to run back into flames to do what, exactly? Does either of you have a plan to fix this, or are you just going to continue passing the blame?"

Bart perched on both hands to lean toward to the group and said, "Well, let me tell everyone in this room something: The blame stops here! We are going to come out of this meeting with a single voice and a single plan. We are going to work *with* each other and not *against* each other."

"Why should I carry weak team members?" Ms. Rays demanded.

"If the deployment team did their job, this wouldn't have happened in the first place," Mr. Stone, the vice president from Client Services, responded.

Ashlie said, "Mr. Stone, do you know what the deployment team does?"

"No," he answered. "It's not my area."

"He's right," Mr. Mavee said. "Why should he have to know what Tommy is supposed to do?"

"I'll tell you why," Bart responded. "But first I'm going to answer Ms. Rays. The *reason* you should carry another department is that we are all in this together. If another division is failing repeatedly, then we need to work with HR to address the issue, but we will always carry the weaker teams until they are either stronger or carrying us. This is a team effort, not every person for themselves. Now to answer Mr. Stone, as a member of our team, you need to know what the other divisions are accountable for. Especially if you are going to make accusations about their performance. So, at this time, I would ask that Mr. Mavee, Ms. Rays, and Mr. Stone come with me and Alexa and Ashlie to the neighboring meeting room to further discuss a few things. As for the rest of the room, please help yourselves to the refreshments, but don't wander off."

The room became quiet as the attendees watched Bart, then the troublesome trio, then Alexa and Ashlie exit the room.

Bart asked Mr. Mavee to join Alexa in her office, Ms. Rays to join him and Ashlie in Ashlie's office, and Mr. Stone to have a seat in a nearby meeting room with assurances that they would be right with him.

Once the group in Ashlie's office sat down, Bart asked Ms. Rays, "Are you willing to adopt a more team-oriented attitude and accept some additional responsibility to help right this ship?"

Ms. Rays retorted, "I am the vice president of Programming, and we as an organization live and breathe on what *my* group does. We need stronger leaders to right this ship or you're all going down with it." She went on explaining her importance to the company and how she was not willing to collaborate with other groups since her group was more important.

Bart excused himself and Ashlie for a quick chat in the hall. After a short conversation, he headed into Alexa's office to meet with her and Mr. Mavee.

Taking a seat next to Alexa, Bart asked, "Mr. Mavee, can you tell me how you feel the yearly project is going and your take on our leadership team?"

Mr. Mavee replied, "It should be obvious; your leadership team is in real trouble. It can't lead, and the project is failing because people don't do what they're told." He leaned forward to emphasize his next statement to Bart. "You have *got* to toughen up and cut lose your dead weight."

Bart asked how Mr. Mavee would handle this situation, and after listening to Mr. Mavee's plan to get things on track, he asked him to hold tight and for Alexa to join him in the meeting room with Mr. Stone.

Mr. Stone stood and shook both Bart's and Alexa's hand when they entered. Bart asked him the same questions he had asked Ms. Rays and Mr. Mavee. The answers from Mr. Stone were very different in that he was very supportive and humble. He went on to explain that he trusted the other leaders and believed in open debate. He had been honest when he'd made the statement about not knowing what Tommy's group did and admittedly felt his comment was not in line with the spirit of the organization and must have come from frustration, and he then offered both Bart and Alexa a sincere apology.

Tommy suggested everyone grab their laptops and make use of the wait time to work through their constant tidal wave of incoming e-mails while they had a break in the action. An hour later, Bart returned to the conference room with only Mr. Stone, inspiring a few shared glances around the table.

Bart walked to the front of the room. "Are you ready to start up again?"

Joy, one of the other senior leaders in the room, noticed the group was missing a few people as Bart returned. She asked, "Are the others joining us?"

Bart took a seat and replied, "Mr. Mavee and Ms. Rays are no longer employed at Sanitas Est. I'm serious about fixing things, and we need to work together in order to do that. If there's anyone who wants out, speak up. I'll offer you six month's severance, and you can walk away."

Everyone looked around the room.

One person in the back said, "I'll take it!" and began to exit with Alexa close behind.

Bart thanked the individual for their honesty and said he would visit with them soon.

"Now for the rest of us. Welcome to Day One."

CHAPTER 14
THE TASTE OF HUMBLE PIE

The following week it seemed like there was electricity flowing through the halls as the watercooler talk buzzed with the news of Mr. Mavee's and Ms. Rays's departures. Senior executives were booked for one-on-ones with Bart all throughout the first part of the week. Tommy and Bart worked at a steady pace with other leaders within the organization on how they could apply their four-step process company-wide in preparation for a company meeting they would hold the following week, with video conferencing for their remote employees.

When the big morning for the company meeting arrived, everyone onsite waited in the largest conference room while offsite employees streamed the meeting live to their desktops. Bart and Tommy were stationed in another meeting room, from where they would broadcast live to everyone. At exactly 9:30 a.m., Bart stepped up to the microphone. Every room was silent as he began, as if screen prompts had flashed telling people to hold their breath and not make a sound.

"First off, I want to thank you for coming this morning. From what I understand, some of you have turned in your departure notices and are only with us for a short time longer. Some have already left. I would like to start by saying, I'm sorry. I hope you will all forgive those that followed my instructions to make the organizational changes like we did as well. I take responsibility for what has happened around here the last few months."

The view on the monitors everyone was watching was of a caring and empathetic person speaking from the heart. On the sidelines around Bart, the senior leaders were poised and relaxed and appeared to be operating as a single unit as they nodded in agreement while Bart spoke.

The employees began to breathe again and relaxed in their seats.

Bart continued the meeting by thanking key members and discussing what his intentions were and were not. He said he wanted to be clear that this was a learning opportunity for everyone involved. As the meeting was nearing Bart's self-imposed transition point, he said he wanted everyone to know he had a plan he would be sharing so the company could move forward. "My intentions are to get this once-thriving company back in order by entrusting my leaders and staff. I will be here to guide the teams and make sure the process is the same and conforms across the company," he said. "I take full responsibility for the lack of consistent direction and want to assure everyone that I will do my best to make sure everyone has clear and consistent actions. I understand there have been hours of unpaid overtime put in for this release by our salaried staff, which I'm thankful for, and I am planning a company event with awards and prizes for those who help us finish this project once we have the new dates."

Next, Bart mentioned changes in some of the company's leadership positions and that the consultant they had hired, Mr. Mavee, was no longer with the organization.

As if on cue, laughs and applause erupted throughout the halls and cubicle forest.

Lastly, before he handed the mic over to other leaders, he reminded everyone he was thankful for them and said, "I will do my best to make Sanitas Est a wonderful place to be."

The meeting rooms came alive with claps and whistles. Bart

looked over at Tommy, who gestured like Bart's zipper was down. Bart glanced down in shock, then smiled at Tommy's prank.

Tommy and other managers followed with the same unified message. They announced there would be meetings with each team over the next few days and that anyone who had turned in their notice earlier in the week could recall it with HR with no hard feelings.

As the meeting drew to a close, Bart again took the podium to make one final announcement. "I hope the meeting today and the one-on-ones in the coming days will convince you all to stay. I would like to say I'm putting the yearly release project on hold. During this hold, we will review the affected areas of business and determine what needs attention quickly." After one more round of thank-yous to everyone, the meeting came to a close.

The room and remote locations broke into a steady wave of clapping one last time as Bart and his team exited the main stage.

Throughout the next two days, Tommy hosted planning and strategy meetings with his departments and other divisions within the company, including the offshore groups and HR. By Friday, he was wrapping up his to-do list in his office, and for the first time in some while, the tide of e-mails from frustrated business partners clogging his inbox had subsided, so that he was preparing to put the week behind him. As he was straightening up, he noticed a card sitting on the far corner of his desk. He hesitated to open it; his wrap-up of the week had been going well, and he wasn't sure he wanted to open a new can of worms right before heading home. Tommy sat back in his chair and took a deep breath in anticipation of bad news. Picking up the envelope, he noticed his trademark yellow smiley on the front. As he began to open it, a feeling of pride and thankfulness welled up inside him. The card was from his delivery team and expressed thanks, saying they would pass on the happy hour and dinner because they believed he had delivered on what he pledged. There were many signatures and a special note from Michael saying he was disappointed that Tommy didn't get a raise for all his trouble.

He felt that constituted a "disappointment," so he should still get his happy hour.

Tommy closed his laptop and packed his papers and the card into his bag to head home. As he climbed into his truck, he wondered what Mazi was doing this weekend. It dawned on him that he was enjoying having her around on the weekends and that she had been partly responsible for giving him time to focus on work recently by keeping Bryan busy and checking his homework.

When Tommy pulled off the road onto his gravel drive, he noticed Hank was at the gate waiting for Bryan. He decided to get out and wait for the bus with him. Soon it arrived, and with an explosion, Bryan leaped from his yellow chariot with carrots in one hand, like the swords of a gladiator but eight inches long and orange. In his other hand, he grasped a small bag of green cubes from the feed store. The boy declared, "There's my buddy," but Tommy did not know if he was addressing him or Hank.

That night Mazi came to visit her parents and "check on the boys." Tommy offered to practice his cooking skills on her if she would join them. She agreed so long as Bryan could go with her to the feed store again.

Later that evening over dinner, Tommy asked Mazi if she had thought about coming back to live in the area. He mentioned that Vanesa was happy having her around and maybe he could hire her to watch Bryan. She smiled, and Bryan fired off a kick in his dad's direction under the table, adding, "I don't need a babysitter." As dinner went on, Bryan recounted the many cool things he'd found at the feed store while he was out with Mazi.

Later, after Bryan was tucked in for the night, the adults sat on the porch and discussed how work had been progressing. They also talked about how Bryan was becoming focused and happy again.

"The last few months have been difficult, but I'm happy with the direction we're headed in," said Tommy. "It would be nice to have you around more than just on the weekends, but I understand your job is kinda far from here and it would be a long daily commute."

"It'll only be a few more years before I can get my own veterinarian clinic, unless you decide to use those business skills and put a clinic nearby," she joked.

It was getting late, so Mazi said good night and Tommy offered to walk her home. She smiled and said, "I'll be fine. I know the way down this path."

"At the very least, let me get you a flashlight," he offered.

"All right, then," she said.

Tommy retrieved the flashlight for Mazi, then watched her walk down the lane. He followed the light through the woods, losing it a few times in the dense foliage. Soon the phone rang, and Mazi let him know she was home. They said good night and hung up.

When the phone rang the next morning, Tommy froze for a moment, hoping it wasn't the office. Eventually, he answered, relieved to hear Vanesa's voice inviting him and Bryan to breakfast. Tommy had learned not to try getting out of it when Vanesa wanted their company, so he rousted Bryan and they walked over. As Don opened the door for them, the smell of fresh biscuits and bacon filled the air. Over breakfast, Tommy dropped the news that Mazi would come home if he opened her a vet clinic.

Boom! Now she kicked him under the table.

This kicking is becoming a regular thing, he thought.

"Really?" Vanesa looked surprised. "We have been trying for years to get her back, and all it would cost us is a little clinic."

"No, Mom. Tommy and I were just discussing that you and Dad are getting older."

"No, we weren't," Tommy denied. Now he was doing the kicking, and Bryan was laughing.

"Well, we mentioned you liked having me here. I told Tommy if I get my own clinic, I *might* consider coming back someday."

Everyone laughed and talked about their week, enjoying the time together and the delicious country breakfast Vanesa had made for them. After breakfast, Vanesa and Tommy sat on the porch and she asked him how work was going. He replied that work was a mess, but they were now moving in the right direction.

"How about Bryan?" she asked.

"He's back to usual in school and doing very well at keeping up with his chores and projects around the house," Tommy said. "Seems that before long, things will be back to normal once again."

Vanessa gave him a conspiratorial grin and said, "So how are things with you and Mazi?"

He wasn't ready for this direct question, but smiled and said, "Maybe she is developing intentions on opening her own clinic."

"Her intentions?," Vanesa said.

"Yep, just like Don needed help to find his intentions, right?" Tommy said, beaming.

CHAPTER 15
DELIVERY

At Monday's team meeting, everyone was eager to hear what Tommy had to say. He entered the room to a few smiling faces and a few that looked uncertain, but at least everyone was there. He moved with a new pep to his step and happily tossed out a quick introduction: "Hey, guys, I know you've heard it before, but I wanted to again thank you for being here and for all that you have contributed." After providing the team a clear understanding of Bart's intentions for the company, he laid out his intentions and described how the departments under his management were going to fit into the larger picture.

During this process, Tommy explained he would meet with other leaders to help them better define their actions at the departmental level. He put a slide up on the projector defining four steps they would follow and explained it was everyone's responsibility to keep the team on track. The group went over the four steps, discussing with each step how it applied to their roles and responsibilities.

- **Announce your intentions** – Let others know your goals and what you expect.
- **Be consistent with your actions** – Show you are sound in your conviction by demonstrating to others you have a direction and encourage them to come along.

- **Reward positive behavior** – Acknowledge and reward when you see positive behavior.
- **Reflection** – Review what worked and what to improve in the future.

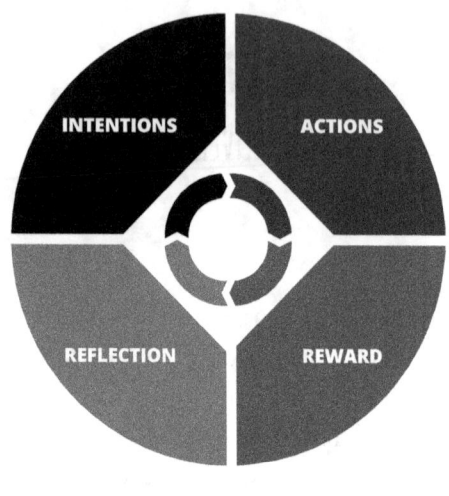

A few weeks passed, and the delivery group had helped polish the actions section for the yearly release project. New delivery dates were mapped to a realistic timeline and a new budget was approved that took into account what would be needed to ensure quality code and on-time delivery.

The delivery team agreed on the following plan for their department goals.

- **Announce your intentions** – Deliver the annual project with clean, bug-free software to the production environment by June 1.
- **Be consistent with your actions** – Provide a weekly update via a dashboard to display progress that's been made and call out any roadblocks.
- **Reward positive behavior** – The contributing departments and the delivery team will receive a reward

for early delivery that is complete, bug-free, and able to be moved into production.
- **Reflection** – The delivery team's leadership and project leads will meet every other Thursday to review the project and make changes as needed.

The next weekend, Tommy announced he was planning a dinner for the Levis and asked Mazi to join them at a little neighborhood diner just down the road. The business was a hobby venture for their neighbors, the Greens, who seemed to like starting businesses more than running them.

When he arrived at dinner, Tommy was all smiles and goofing around with Bryan. The group was seated in a private dining area and served a variety of delicious "home cooking," followed by their choice of three desserts. Ms. Green visited the group and inquired about the occasion as they enjoyed the spread.

"We are here so I can repay some of the many meals Ms. Vanesa has shared with us, along with her wisdom to help me refocus my personal and professional life," Tommy explained. "I also wanted to make sure I would be invited back to the Levis' house, so I opted to not cook for them myself."

Ms. Green offered her congratulations and then said she and her husband were looking forward to their move back to the West Coast.

Vanesa was shocked to hear they were moving. She had heard rumors that they were looking to sell the property, which included their large farmhouse up on the hill, the building they were eating in, and the land in between.

"Who bought it?" Vanesa asked.

"Well, I'd thought that's why you're here," smiled Ms. Green.

Tommy turned a little red. "Well, I guess I was going to ask you some time. It doesn't look like I'm going to be right next door much longer," he said, smiling at Mazi. "I have something to ask Mazi. Well, here goes."

Mazi looked like she was going to faint.

"Mazi, can we adopt Hank?"

"Aww," Mazi said, slapping his leg.

Ms. Vanesa let out a little "whew," and they all laughed.

Tommy then explained that the lease was coming up on his house and, with his job going so well, he couldn't imagine moving away. The new house had lots of land, barns, and a pond. He was only concerned with what to do with the little building on the road front, explaining that the Greens were taking all the restaurant equipment to open a place out west. It seems that was why they had been testing their different little business ideas all along, and they'd finally found one they liked. The gains from the sale were going to finance their newest adventure.

Vanesa said, "If only someone had intentions of starting a little business and renting the house next door to us, then the neighborhood would be full again."

Mazi gave everyone a playful glare at being entangled in some conspiracy.

CHAPTER 16
STATE YOUR INTENTIONS

THE NEXT FEW WEEKS WERE busy but fulfilling. Tommy's mornings had adjusted back to a pleasant cadence, allowing him to wait with Bryan and Hank at the end of the driveway. At the office, he was attending more executive functions and becoming a regular in board meeting discussions.

At the quarterly Board of Directors meeting, Tommy was asked to be a guest speaker and provide outlines and in-depth explanations about the methods he'd used to help refocus the company. During his presentation, Tommy committed to supporting Bart's intentions for organizational growth and providing a reliable set of actions to follow.

When the meeting ended, Bart asked Tommy to visit him in his office at about 3 p.m.

"Don't tell me you're going to fire me now," Tommy poked.

"Maybe someday, but probably not today." Bart retorted.

As Tommy approached his boss's door later that afternoon, he noticed Ashlie and Alexa sitting next to Bart's desk and a single chair directly in front of it. For a slight second, he felt a tinge of worry and wondered, *What have I done?* Then a wave of confidence flooded over him and he walked through the door, confident he had done well and was ready to discuss whatever they wanted to meet about.

Bart smiled as he stood to shake Tommy's hand. "Sir, you have really been busy around here."

Tommy gave Bart a firm handshake and then a noticeable glance at his zipper before he went to take his seat.

Bart looked down at his zipper, then back at Tommy with a wide grin.

Ashlie and Alexa looked in their own laps, trying to figure out what the boys were joking about.

Bart saw their confusion and explained, "Tommy likes to trick me that my zipper is down. At some point I explained to Tommy that a friend would tell you if your zipper were down in private and not in public, so as to help you be the best you can be. In private they may razz you. It is a way of providing constructive criticism and to help us remember we can all benefit from advice from time to time, no matter what our position in life or business may be."

The ladies blushed, and everyone laughed.

"Have a seat, and let's discuss something," Bart said to Tommy.

The meeting with Bart and HR did not take very long, though it did leave Tommy a little shell-shocked. He gathered up his laptop from his office and made his way home before the afternoon traffic could offer him extra time to enjoy the view alongside the expressway.

As Tommy pulled off the main road, he noticed Hank was on his way down to the gate and decided to visit with the gentle giant while waiting on Bryan's bus. He made his way over to the fence and offered a hand to pet him. "Now don't be getting any flashbacks and decide to bite me for old time's sake," he quipped.

Hank approached the edge of his boundary and encouraged Tommy to rub his head. The fragrance of fresh cut hay, honeysuckle, and the outdoors always gave Tommy a tranquil feeling.

As if on cue, the big yellow bus pulled up at the end of the driveway and Bryan shot out the door. He dashed up to hug Tommy and then offered Hank his reward for being there to walk him home. He looked up at his dad and said, "What's up? You here to visit with Hank too?"

"No," Tommy replied. "I got off work early for a change and wanted to wait for you. Want a ride up to the house?"

"No way. This is Hank's and my time. He would feel cheated if he didn't get to walk me home."

Tommy watched as Bryan approached Hank with his special treats and offered them up one at a time while rubbing his muzzle.

"Here you go, Hank, thanks for being here, you big smelly. Wait, hey, Dad, can we give Hank a bath?" Bryan's turbocharged thought process jumped into overdrive.

Tommy tousled Bryan's hair, saying, "No bath tonight for Hank, and don't venture off or go exploring because Mazi is coming for dinner."

"Yay!" Bryan said, bounding off to race Hank back to the barn.

Tommy headed home and started preparing dinner. Mazi arrived to check on the boys and discuss the move in their near future. Bryan showed up with dirty knees right before dinner was served. Mazi found it amusing to watch Tommy ask what had happened and Bryan shrug while giving his patented, "What?" Tommy sent the boy upstairs to clean up, telling him to hustle because dinner was ready.

Over dinner, Tommy produced a manila envelope and sat it in the middle of the table. Everyone stared at it silently for a moment. Slowly, like a snake, Bryan reached for the new object now acting as a centerpiece. He slyly peeled back the opening and peered inside. With a puzzled look, he removed the documents and began reading out loud.

"Mr. Divers, as a token of our thanks, please enjoy two weeks in Paris to acquaint yourself with our clients there. I'm sure they would love to congratulate you on your promotion. P.S. Please let us know the name of the person who will be traveling with you so we may book your travels. Sincerely, Ashlie."

Bryan looked up and asked, "Am I going to Paris?"

"Well, I was wondering if I could take someone else," Tommy said with a wink.

"Who?" Bryan asked.

"I was thinking of taking you," Tommy said, pointing to Mazi. From under the table, he produced a travel guide to France and handed it to Mazi, offering a boyish grin to seal the deal.

"Really?" Mazi said, wide-eyed and grinning ear to ear.

"Oh, I almost forgot." Tommy jumped up, went to his attaché, produced a pocket-sized book titled *Starting Your Own Business*, and placed it next to her as well. "I thought you might like to read this on the plane. It might inspire you."

She grinned and kissed him on the cheek.

Bryan covered his eyes. "Ewww! No kissing!"

ACKNOWLEDGEMENTS

I would like to thank my very patient girlfriend and partner in crime, Dejane Kerr. She has shown enormous patience with my daily antics and inability to grow up. A well-deserved mention is to the team at The Pro Book Editor for their guidance and support.

ABOUT THE AUTHOR

Charlie Kesinger is an accomplished transformational leader who enjoys a variety of activities. His portfolio of achievements includes business, friendships, and a passion for having fun with life. Charlie's broad background encompasses an exceptional work ethic and commitment to find the best in others.

In 2015, he took his passion for helping people to a new level by pursuing a Ph.D. in Organizational Leadership focusing on Social Identity Theory. He previously attended Northwestern University to obtain a Master of Science degree (Medical Informatics). His undergrad is in Business Administration, but his best education has come from life experiences and face to face interactions.

www.ingramcontent.com/pod-product-compliance
Lightning Source LLC
Chambersburg PA
CBHW052100070526
44584CB00017B/2273